G000069555

FOOD LABELLING: THE FDA'S ROLE IN THE SELECTION OF HEALTHY FOODS

FOOD AND BEVERAGE CONSUMPTION AND HEALTH SERIES

Handbook of Green Tea and Health Research
Helen McKinley and Mark Jamieson (Editors)
2009. ISBN: 978-1-60741-045-4

Marketing Food to Children and Adolescents
Nicoletta A. Wilks
2009 ISBN: 978-1-60692-913-1

Food Labelling: The FDA's Role in the Selection of Healthy Foods
Ethan C. Lefevre (Editor)
2009. ISBN: 78-1-60692-898-1

Food and Beverage Consumption and Health

FOOD LABELLING: THE FDA'S ROLE IN THE SELECTION OF HEALTHY FOODS

ETHAN C. LEFEVRE
EDITOR

Nova Science Publishers, Inc.
New York

LIBRARY OF CONGRESS CATALOGING-IN-PUBLICATION DATA
Available upon request
ISBN: 978-1-60692-898-1

Published by Nova Science Publishers, Inc. ✦ New York

CONTENTS

Preface   **vii**

Chapter 1   Food Labelling: FDA Needs to Better
                 Leverage Resources, Improve Oversight,
                 and Effectively Use Available Data
                 to Help Consumers Select Healthy Foods   **1**
                 United States Government Accountability Office

Chapter 2   Food and Drug Administration (FDA):
                 Overview and Issues   **71**
                 Erin D. Williams

Index   **81**

PREFACE

Two thirds of U.S. adults are overweight, and childhood obesity and diabetes are on the rise. To reverse these health problems, experts are urging Americans to eat healthier. Food labels contain information to help consumers who want to make healthy food choices. The Food and Drug Administration (FDA) oversees federal labeling rules for 80 percent of foods. This book explores Food Labelling in the U.S., wherein the FDA needs to better leverage resources, improve oversight and effectively use available data to help consumers select healthy foods. FDA's oversight and enforcement efforts have not kept pace with the growing number of food firms. As a result, FDA has little assurance that companies comply with food labeling laws and regulations for, among other things, preventing false or misleading labeling. FDA has reported that limited resources and authorities challenge its efforts to carry out its food safety responsibilities— these challenges also impact efforts to oversee food labeling laws. As discussed in this book, the FDA's Food Protection Plan cites the need for authority to, among other things, collect a reinspection user fee, accredit third-party inspectors, and require recalls when voluntary recalls are not effective.

Chapter 1 - FDA has limited assurance that domestic and imported foods comply with food labeling requirements, such as those prohibiting false or misleading labeling. This is because, while the number of food firms has increased annually, the number of inspections, warning letters, and most enforcement actions to address violations, has decreased or remained steady

Chapter 2 - The Food and Drug Administration (FDA) is the agency within the Department of Health and Human Services (HHS) that regulates human and animal drugs, medical devices, biologics, and most foods. This report describes FDA, surveys agency-related issues Congress faces, and cites CRS reports where readers can find more information.

In: Food Labelling: FDA's Role...
Editor: Ethan C. Lefevre, pp. 1-69

ISBN 978-1-60692-898-1
© 2009 Nova Science Publishers, Inc.

Chapter 1

FOOD LABELLING: FDA NEEDS TO BETTER LEVERAGE RESOURCES, IMPROVE OVERSIGHT, AND EFFECTIVELY USE AVAILABLE DATA TO HELP CONSUMERS SELECT HEALTHY FOODS[*]

United States Government Accountability Office

ABBREVIATIONS

AMA	American Medical Association
CFSAN	Center for Food Safety and Applied Nutrition
FACTS	Field Accomplishments and Compliance Tracking System
FDA	Food and Drug Administration
FSIS	Food Safety and Inspection Service
FTC	Federal Trade Commission
FTE	full-time-equivalent
HHS	Department of Health and Human Services
mg	milligram
NLEA	Nutrition Labeling and Education Act

---

[*] Excerpted from GAO Report 08-597 to the Chair, Subcommittee on Agriculture, Rural Development, Food and Drug Administration, and Related Agencies, Committee on Appropriations, House of Representatives, dated September 2009.

OASIS   Operational and Administrative System for Import Support
ORA   Office of Regulatory Affairs
RES   Recall Enterprise System
USDA   U.S. Department of Agriculture

September 9, 2008

The Honorable Rosa DeLauro Chair
Subcommittee on Agriculture, Rural Development,
Food and Drug Administration, and Related Agencies
Committee on Appropriations House of Representatives

Dear Madam Chair:

Two thirds of U.S. adults are overweight, and the incidence of childhood obesity and diabetes has been rising. In an effort to reverse these growing public health problems, medical professionals are encouraging Americans to eat healthier, more nutritious foods. In 2005, the Department of Health and Human Services (HHS) and the U.S. Department of Agriculture (USDA) issued Dietary Guidelines for Americans. These guidelines and the food guide pyramid, [1] developed by USDA to visually convey the guidelines and other nutrition information, help policy makers design and implement nutrition-related programs. Federal agencies must promote this guidance in carrying out federal food, nutrition, or health programs; meals served under the school lunch program must be consistent with the guidance. This guidance provides science-based dietary direction for consumers to limit their sugar, fat, and salt; eat more whole grains, fruits, and vegetables; and monitor portion size. According to the guidance, a healthy diet reduces the risk for chronic diseases, such as heart disease, certain cancers, diabetes, and stroke—all major causes of death and disability in the United States.

Food labels contain information to help consumers who want to follow the dietary guidance and to make healthy food choices that best fit their dietary needs. Within HHS, the Food and Drug Administration (FDA) is responsible for administering federal food labeling requirements, in accordance with the Federal Food, Drug, and Cosmetic Act, as amended [2]. This act prohibits labeling that, among other things, is false or misleading or fails to list the amounts of certain nutrients. When industry, consumer groups, or others believe that certain types of food labeling information is false or misleading, or that changes to requirements are needed for public health, or for other reasons, they may request or formally petition FDA to issue regulations or guidance to address the problem.

FDA oversees industry compliance with the food labeling requirements as part of its food oversight mission. FDA's Center for Food Safety and Applied Nutrition (CFSAN)—one of its six mission centers—is responsible for food, cosmetics, and related products. Within CFSAN, the Office of Nutrition, Labeling, and Dietary Supplements publishes regulations and guidance on food labeling and provides policy interpretations for overseeing compliance with statutes and regulations that, among others things, prohibit false or misleading labeling. FDA's Office of Regulatory Affairs (ORA) undertakes inspections and enforcement activities for all FDA centers.

FDA's guidance for inspecting domestic or foreign food firms—such as manufacturers, processors, and other food-handling businesses—directs investigators to focus primarily on food safety issues and to review the labels on at least three products during every food safety inspection. To augment its inspection capacity, FDA contracts with states to carry out food safety inspections, following FDA guidance. When FDA inspects food shipments entering the United States from a foreign country, it may also review food labels. To test for the accuracy of labeling information, investigators may send samples of domestic or imported food to FDA laboratories for analysis. FDA also may follow up on complaints from consumers, consumer groups, individual firms, industry groups, or others who believe they have identified food that violates FDA's labeling regulations.

FDA has a number of tools for responding when food labeling violations are identified. It may ask companies to voluntarily recall any food that has already entered the distribution chain. FDA may also send a warning letter to a firm, which is a notice that enforcement actions may be forthcoming if corrections are not made; according to FDA guidance, warning letters are used for serious violations. For less serious violations, FDA may send an untitled letter, which is an informal communication that corrective actions are needed. At any point, FDA may hold a regulatory meeting with the firm to resolve a labeling violation or work with a firm to obtain voluntary compliance. When violations are not corrected, FDA may initiate actions to seize and remove the food from the marketplace (a seizure) or enjoin a firm from continuing a practice that violates food labeling statutes and regulations (an injunction). For food imported from a foreign country, FDA may issue an import refusal to prevent a shipment with a serious labeling violation from entering the United States. FDA may also release a shipment "with comment"—that is, allow the shipment with a labeling violation to enter the United States with notice to the importer that subsequent shipments might be refused entry if the violation is not corrected. In addition, FDA maintains an "import alert" list to detain entries of foreign foods that appear to have significant recurring or unusual violations.

In January 2007, we added federal oversight of food safety to our High-Risk Series, which is intended to raise the priority and visibility of government programs that are in need of broad-based transformation to achieve greater economy, efficiency, effectiveness, accountability, and sustainability [3]. In particular, we have noted that federal expenditures by FDA and USDA for food oversight have not been commensurate with the volume of foods regulated by the agencies or consumed by the public. In November 2007, a report for FDA's Science Board—FDA Science and Mission at Risk—pointed out the erosion in FDA's science base and the inadequacy of FDA's information technology infrastructure [4]. The report cited numerous management challenges that have contributed to FDA's inability to fulfill its mission and that cannot be addressed with available resources. Also in November 2007, FDA issued its Food Protection Plan: An Integrated Strategy for Protecting the Nation's Food Supply (Food Protection Plan), [5] which recognized the need for several changes to ensure the safety of the nation's food supply and identified new authorities needed to implement the new strategy, such as the authority to charge user fees for certain reinspections. In a May 2008 letter (the May 2008 resource needs assessment), FDA's Commissioner identified the resources needed in broad categories to, among other things, begin implementing the Food Protection Plan to protect against new and emerging threats to food safety [6]. We have testified that FDA's plan is a good first step, but pointed out that it does not provide a clear description of resources and strategies that Congress will need to assess the likelihood of the plan's success [7]. Also, with respect to making the most of resources, in May 2008 we issued a special publication entitled Federal User Fees: A Design Guide, which presented various ways to design user fees to encourage greater efficiency, equity, and revenue adequacy and to reduce the administrative burden on the agency and payers of the fees [8].

You asked us to examine (1) FDA's efforts to ensure that domestic and imported foods comply with food labeling requirements, including those prohibiting false or misleading labeling; (2) the challenges FDA faces in its efforts to administer and enforce food labeling requirements; and (3) the actions stakeholders from health, medical, and consumer organizations believe are needed to mitigate the effects of food labeling practices they consider misleading and to help consumers identify healthy food.

For this report, our definition of "food" includes conventional food, dietary supplements, infant formula, and medical food; we excluded animal feed, which the Federal Food, Drug, and Cosmetic Act includes in its definition of food. We did not independently determine whether particular food labels were false or misleading; the examples we cite are food labels that FDA or a health, medical, industry, or consumer group characterized as false or misleading. We also did not evaluate how efficiently FDA used its resources or the impact of changing priorities; nor did we compare FDA resource trends with other federal agencies.

To examine FDA's efforts to ensure that domestic and imported foods comply with food labeling statutes and regulations, we analyzed FDA's and CFSAN's plans and reports; guidance and regulations; and data on labeling-related oversight, enforcement, recalls, warning letters, and complaints. Regarding data for labeling-related oversight, we analyzed the food establishments or facilities (which we call firms) inspected for 7 fiscal years (2001 through 2007); nutrition labeling samples for 7 fiscal years (2000 through 2006); warning letters and enforcement actions related to imports for 6 fiscal years (2002 through 2007); and seizures and injunctions for 10 fiscal years (1998 through 2007)—the periods for which reliable and comparable FDA data were available.

To identify challenges, we reviewed FDA reports and testimonies and analyzed funding and staffing data for FDA, CFSAN, and ORA for 10 fiscal years (1998 through 2007) and the Office of Nutrition, Labeling, and Dietary Supplements, which began maintaining comparable data in 1999, for 9 fiscal years (1999 through 2007). We also reviewed FDA oversight and enforcement authorities and court rulings regarding FDA labeling. For comparison, we examined similar information for USDA's Food Safety and Inspection Service (FSIS) and the Federal Trade Commission (FTC), which also oversee and enforce requirements related to food labeling. For stakeholder positions, we analyzed the views of health, medical, consumer, and industry groups obtained from interviews and documents, such as reports and petitions.

We assessed the reliability of the data used in this report and found it to be sufficiently reliable for the purposes used. We conducted this performance audit from January 2007 through September 2008 in accordance with generally accepted government auditing standards. Those standards require that we plan and perform the audit to obtain sufficient, appropriate evidence to provide a reasonable basis for our findings and conclusions based on our audit objectives. We believe that the evidence obtained provides a reasonable basis for our findings and conclusions based on our audit objectives.

Appendix I contains more detailed information on our objectives, scope, and methodology.

RESULTS IN BRIEF

FDA has limited assurance that domestic and imported foods comply with food labeling requirements, such as those prohibiting false or misleading labeling. This is because, while the number of food firms has increased annually, the number of inspections, warning letters, and most enforcement actions to address violations, has decreased or remained steady. Specifically, we found the following:

- *Label reviews*: Although FDA guidance directs investigators to review labels on at least three food products when inspecting domestic and foreign firms, FDA has no reliable data on the number of labels that were actually reviewed. Moreover, the number of inspections of food firms has not kept pace with the growth in firms from 2001 through 2007. The number of domestic firms under FDA's jurisdiction increased from about 51,000 to more than 65,000, while the number of firms inspected declined slightly, from 14,721 to 14,566. FDA has inspected few foreign firms, while the number of imported food lines has increased. For example, during 2007, the United States imported food from tens of thousands of foreign food firms in more than 150 countries yet FDA inspected only 96 firms in 11 countries. In addition, FDA's limited sampling of inspected food to test for the accuracy of nutrient information on labels found high error rates for certain nutrients.
- *Communications:* The number of warning letters FDA issued to firms that included food labeling violations has held relatively steady since 2002, while the total number of letters decreased by nearly half—from 806 in 2002 to 434 in 2007. However, official data on warning letters may also be incomplete. In addition, FDA does not track the number of regulatory meetings initiated by its field offices for labeling violations, and it does not know whether the field offices are using the same criteria for these meetings.
- *Enforcement actions*: FDA has initiated actions resulting in 21 seizures and 2 injunctions for food labeling violations, since 1998. FDA also has refused entry to an average of about 2,500 food product lines, annually, that had food labeling violations, since 2002. In addition, as of January 2008, FDA had 64 active import alerts for labeling violations.

Moreover, FDA does not provide its managers with routine reports on, for example, (1) the status of labeling violations to help them ensure that corrections are made quickly and properly and (2) trends in labeling violations by types of products, companies, and countries to help inform their decisions for setting priorities and allocating resources. In addition, FDA does not ensure that the information it posts on its public Web site— such as warning letters that identify labeling violations—is complete and posted promptly to inform consumers' food purchase decisions. Furthermore, CFSAN continues to maintain a duplicate database of firms' food recalls that FDA had agreed to eliminate in response to our 2004 recommendation [9].

FDA has reported that limited resources and authorities significantly challenge its efforts to carry out food safety responsibilities—challenges that also impact efforts to administer and enforce labeling requirements. Specifically, we found the following:

- *Resources:* From 1999 through 2007, funding and staffing for CFSAN's Office of Nutrition, Labeling, and Dietary Supplements rose and fell several times. Funding fluctuated from $6.8 million to $10.0 million and staffing from 65 to 88 full-time-equivalent (FTE) staff. In 2007, funding of $8.2 million was its lowest since 2001, and staffing of 65 FTEs was a 9-year low. However, the portion of that office's funding and staffing dedicated to food labeling activities has held fairly constant since 2005— with funding rising from $1.1 million to $1.3 million and staffing from 9.0 to 10.5 FTEs. In addition, officials told us FDA does not have the resources to conduct the substantial additional research on consumer perceptions necessary to demonstrate that a food label is misleading.

- *Authority:* FDA's Food Protection Plan notes that certain authorities are not available to most food programs that could allow FDA to maximize resources—authorities that could also facilitate labeling oversight. The plan seeks, among other things, authority to charge user fees for reinspecting firms that had violated important requirements; accredit qualified third parties to conduct certain types of reviews and inspections; and mandate food recalls if necessary, which it may do for infant formula and certain medical products. Such authorities currently help other regulatory agencies and are maintained by other FDA mission centers. As FDA pursues new statutory authority for user fees, it could benefit from information in GAO's Federal User Fees: A Design Guide to, among other things, ensure optimal efficiency and minimal burden [10]. Regarding accrediting third parties, FDA could benefit from lessons learned in other FDA programs that use third parties to leverage inspection resources.

Stakeholders we interviewed—including key health, medical, and consumer organizations—identified several actions that they believe will mitigate misleading labeling and help consumers identify healthy food. For example, according to many, consumers find the range of information on labels confusing and misleading. To help consumers more easily and quickly identify healthy food, many stakeholders in the United States and overseas support the addition of a uniform system of symbols on the frontof-package labels to indicate nutritional quality. The National Academies' Institute of Medicine recommended in 2006 that industry, government, scientists, and consumer groups jointly develop such a system. Other countries, such as the United Kingdom and Sweden have developed voluntary nutrition symbol systems, and Canada is consulting with stakeholders and proposing research on front-of-package nutrition symbols. The European Commission has proposed a system for mandatory front-of-package nutrition labeling. FDA held a public hearing in 2007 to solicit comments on front-of-package nutrition symbols and has begun researching this approach.

We are recommending seven actions that FDA should take to (1) ensure that labeling office managers have the information they need to oversee compliance with food labeling laws and regulations; (2) ensure that the public has timely access to information on food labeling violations that may have serious health consequences on FDA's public Web site; and (3) better leverage resources to carry out food-related mission responsibilities, including developing detailed information on how the new authorities it seeks would help it achieve its mission, and evaluating options for conveying nutritional quality that will mitigate consumer confusion and misleading labeling.

In commenting on a draft of our report, FDA stated that the report raised some important issues regarding its regulation of food labeling and it did not dispute the report's data, analyses, or findings. It commented, however, that the report inappropriately references food labeling as part of its food safety mission, although it acknowledges that there may be some aspects of food labeling that can affect the safe use of food. That notwithstanding, FDA requires investigators to review at least three labels during food safety inspections. FDA also stated that within its overall public health mission, it has a multitude of competing priorities. We acknowledged FDA's competing priorities in the report's conclusions and framed the recommendations so as to help manage these competing priorities by better leveraging resources and using available tools and data for risk- based decisions.

With respect to our recommendations, FDA generally agreed with some, but with qualifications. Regarding our recommendations that FDA ensure managers have information they need for effective food labeling oversight by maintaining and analyzing data they need on violations in routine reports, FDA agreed that being able to track any and all information that would allow investigators to better do their jobs would be useful to the agency. However, FDA stated that data collection requires time and effort and it is important to make sure that data entry does not become so burdensome that it takes away from other investigative work. FDA did not commit to taking any actions in response to these recommendations. We maintain that FDA cannot make risk-based decisions, including resource allocation decisions, effectively without analyzing the detailed food labeling data that the agency has collected for many years. Regarding our recommendation that FDA provide timely and complete data for consumers on its public Web site, FDA said that it already does post and maintain much of the information. However, as our report points out, FDA did not post warning letters promptly and had no assurance that the posted data on food labeling violations were accessible. In addition, consumers should receive complete and timely information and statistics to inform their food purchase decisions. Regarding our recommendation on collaboration with federal agencies and other stakeholders to evaluate labeling options, FDA provided information on the focus of its current research and identified many aspects of symbols that it intends to research. However, a broad research agenda will likely require extensive resources over several years. We considered FDA's competing resource demands when we developed our last recommendation—to better leverage those resources by collaborating with other federal agencies and stakeholders who may be able to contribute resources in the form of staff or funding. Finally, FDA did not comment on our recommendations related to tracking regulatory meetings, providing Congress with information on the new authorities requested in the Food Protection Plan, and posting updates of the status of implementation of this plan on FDA's public Web site.

BACKGROUND

The Federal Food, Drug, and Cosmetic Act, as amended, prohibits the "misbranding" of food, which includes, among other things, labeling that is false or misleading. In 1990, Congress amended the act to mandate that certain nutrition information be provided on packaged foods in a specified, standardized format—only recently have other countries, such as Canada, initiated mandatory nutrition labeling. The act, and FDA regulations implementing it, require food labels to include nutrient, ingredient, and other important content information that consumers can use to make healthy dietary choices, and to avoid allergens (such as peanuts) and other ingredients (such as sulfites) that can cause life-threatening reactions in people who are sensitive to them. For example, the act and FDA's regulations, with some exceptions, [11] require that food labels include the following:

- a Nutrition Facts panel that identifies the serving size; the number of servings per container; the number of calories per serving; and the amount of certain nutrients, such as fiber, vitamins, fat, and sodium; [12]
- an ingredients list that identifies the product's ingredients by their common or usual names, in order of predominance by weight;
- the required information in English; [13] and
- a declaration of the source (e.g., tree nuts) of major allergens.

Figure 1 depicts an example of a Nutrition Facts panel from FDA's regulations illustrating nutrition information and visual display.

Source: FDA.

Figure 1. FDA Example of a Nutrition Facts Panel.

The act and FDA regulations also require that health claims—that is, claims characterizing the relationship of certain nutrients to a disease or a health- related condition—on food labels be authorized by FDA. For example, a main dish that contains 140 milligrams (mg) or less of sodium per 100 grams may be labeled with the claim that "diets low in sodium may reduce the risk of high blood pressure, a disease associated with many factors," provided there are no nutrients in the food at levels that would disqualify it from making this claim. In regulations, FDA has authorized the use of claims for 12 relationships between a nutrient and a disease or health- related condition.

For purposes of compliance, with certain exceptions, a food is subject to enforcement action under FDA regulations if the number of calories or the amount of certain nutrients, such as fat and sugar, is more than 20 percent over the amount declared in the Nutrition Facts panel. The Institute of Medicine established the reference nutrient values that FDA used (along with the Dietary Guidelines for Americans) to establish the daily values for nutrients on the Nutrition Facts panel. In addition, for compliance and enforcement purposes, the amount of certain nutrients naturally occurring in the food must be at least equal to 80 percent of the value declared on the label; the amount of added nutrients in fortified or fabricated foods must be at least equal to the amount shown on the panel. According to FDA, these variations are allowed because, for naturally occurring nutrients, values cannot be precisely controlled and depend on weather and soil conditions, among other variables; in addition, values will vary because different laboratories use different methods and testing devices.

FDA's procedures for handling a product complaint require staff to obtain sufficient information from the complainant to evaluate the complaint and determine if it requires follow-up. Also, the complaint is to be documented in the Field Accomplishments and Compliance Tracking System (FACTS). For a food-labeling-related complaint, the information documented in FACTS should include, among other things, any injury, illness, or adverse event that was reported as having occurred as a result of incorrect labeling, and any follow-up actions. Complaints of significant illness or injury must receive immediate and thorough follow-up, while follow-up on those complaints that do not involve injury or illness may be deferred until the next scheduled inspection of the responsible firm, which may be in a few weeks, months, or several years.

Similarly, FTC authorities prohibit unfair or deceptive acts or practices in or affecting commerce, including false or misleading advertising of food products. In some cases, FDA and FTC have certain overlapping jurisdiction for regulating food advertising, labeling, and promotion. In a 1971 memorandum of understanding, the agencies agreed that FTC would exercise primary responsibility for ensuring that food advertising is truthful and not misleading, and that FDA would have primary responsibility for ensuring that food labeling is truthful and not misleading.

FDA Has Limited Assurance That Companies Are Complying with Food Labeling Requirements

FDA's use of oversight and enforcement tools has not kept pace with the growing number of food firms. As a result, FDA has limited assurance that companies in the food industry are in compliance with food labeling requirements, such as those prohibiting false or misleading labeling. FDA's testing of nutrition information has been limited and has found varying degrees of compliance. Actions in response to labeling violations, such as issuing warning letters, have generally decreased or remained steady. In addition, FDA has not analyzed data on labeling violations and follow-up activities to inform its managers or the public. Furthermore, CFSAN has continued to maintain a duplicate food recall system that FDA had agreed to eliminate in response to a recommendation we made in a 2004 report [14].

Food Labeling Oversight Has Not Kept Pace with the Growing Number of Firms

While the number of domestic food firms has increased, FDA has not increased the number of its inspections in response to this increase (see figure 2). Also, FDA does not have reliable data on the total number of labels reviewed because investigators do not have to enter this information into the FACTS database, which documents other inspection details. In the absence of reliable data on the number of labels reviewed, and assuming that investigators were reviewing three labels each time, as FDA officials told us was the common practice, the number of labels reviewed would have declined with the decline in the number of inspections. FDA has conducted few inspections in foreign food firms and that number has declined significantly—from 211 in 26 countries in 2001 to 95 in 11 countries in 2007—even as the United States has received hundreds of thousands of different imported food product entry lines [15] from tens of thousands of foreign food firms in more than 150 countries. (See app. II for information on the number of domestic and foreign food firms inspected under FDA's jurisdiction during fiscal years 2001 through 2007.) Table 1 shows the number of countries and foreign food firms inspected over this period.

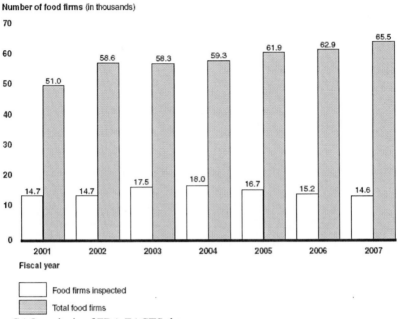

Source: GAO analysis of FDA FACTS data.

Figure 2. Domestic Food Firms under FDA's Jurisdiction and the Number of Firms Inspected by Both FDA and States under Contract with FDA, Fiscal Years 2001 through 2007.

Table 1. The Number of Countries in Which FDA Conducted Inspections and the Number of Foreign Food Firms Inspected, Fiscal Years 2001 through 2007

Foreign inspection	Fiscal Years							
	2001	2002	2003	2004	2005	2006	2007	Total
Number of countries	26	22	22	20	16	15	11	54a
Number of food firms	211	169	148	153	132	125	95	1,034

Source: GAO analysis of FDA data.

[a]The total number of countries was adjusted to count each country only once. FDA had conducted inspections in some countries more than once over the 7-year period.

Appendix III lists the countries and the number of inspections FDA conducted in each country, from fiscal years 2001 through 2007.

In addition, FDA reported inspecting about 1 percent of the different food product entry lines that came into the United States annually during fiscal years 2002 through 2007. However, unlike investigators who perform inspections at manufacturing firms, the investigators who review labels on imported foods are not able to see the manufacturing process, the ingredients stored on shelves, the product formulation, and other documents that provide key information that helps to identify labeling violations.

Testing to Determine the Accuracy of Nutrient Information Is Limited and Outdated, and Shows Varying Degrees of Compliance

While FDA has tested some targeted nonrandom samples of food products to determine the accuracy of nutrition information on their labels, it has tested relatively few food products from some major exporting countries. In addition, FDA has done no random sampling since the 1990s, when some compliance rates varied considerably from the amount identified on the Nutrition Facts panel. From fiscal years 2000 through 2006, FDA collected targeted samples of 868 domestic products and 783 imported products for tests of compliance with nutrition labeling regulations. FDA was unable to provide information on samples taken and test results for fiscal year 2007 because, according to an agency official, the person who analyzed those data had retired from FDA.

According to FDA officials, investigators often selected samples because they noticed obvious labeling violations, such as a candy bar with a Nutrition Facts panel that did not identify any fat or sugar. As table 2 shows, about 21 percent and 28 percent, respectively, of the domestic and imported foods tested were in violation.

The number of samples of imported food FDA has tested for accuracy of nutrition labeling does not relate to the volume of imports or the rate of violations in products from a given country, as table 3 shows. One type of food with a high percentage of violations was infant formula—4 of the 10 formula products sampled were in violation—because they lacked the vitamins, minerals, or other nutrients required by law. While FDA has conducted targeted, nonrandom sampling of labels on imported and domestic food products suspected of having inaccurate information (beyond the allowable ranges) for nutrients listed on their labels, FDA has not conducted random sampling on nutrition labeling since the 1990s.

Table 2. Accuracy of Nutrition Labeling Information for Food Samples Tested, Fiscal Years 2000 through 2006

Fiscal year	Domestic samples			Imported samples			Total domestic and imported samples		
	Number tested	Number in violation	Percentage in violation	Number tested	Number in violation	Percentage in violation	Number tested	Number in violation	Percentage in violation
2000	106	15	14%	150	36	24%	256	51	20%
2001	93	24	26	53	20	38	146	44	30
2002	85	12	14	88	23	26	173	35	20
2003	147	34	23	188	60	32	335	94	28
2004	181	43	24	131	38	29	312	81	26
2005	141	27	19	77	19	25	218	46	21
2006	115	23	20	96	27	28	211	50	24
Total	868	178	21%	783	223	28%	1,651	401	24%

Source: GAO analysis of FDA FACTS data. Note: FDA was unable to provide these data for fiscal year 2007.
Note: FDA was unable to provide these data for fiscal year 2007.

Table 3. The Number of Food Products Tested and Violations Found in Nutrition Facts Panels, Fiscal Years 2000 through 2006, for the Top Nine Countries in Value of Agricultural, Fish, and Seafood Imports

Country (value of agricultural imports for 2006)	Food samples tested, fiscal years 2000-2006		
	Number tested	Number in violation	Percentage inviolation
Canada ($15.6)	93	13	14%
Mexico ($9.8)	200	87	44
Chinaa ($4.2)	26	7	27
Thailand ($3.1)	18	8	44
Italy ($2.8)	31	8	26
Indonesia ($2.8)	2	0	0
Chile ($2.7)	8	2	25
Australia ($2.6)	10	1	10
Brazil ($2.4)	7	4	57

Source: GAO analysis of value of imports data for 2006 from USDA's Foreign Agricultural Service and testing data from FDA's FACTS.

Notes: The country from which a food product was imported may not be the country of origin of the food product. For example, food imported from Canada may have originated in another country.

FDA was unable to provide FACTS sample testing data for fiscal year 2007

[a]The data for China do not include Hong Kong and Macau.

In 1994 and again in 1996, FDA tested 300 randomly selected products to determine the extent to which nutrient information on the Nutrition Facts panel was within the allowable range. According to FDA's analysis of these products, 87 percent (in 1994) and 91 percent (in 1996) of the nutrients were within the allowable range. However, compliance rates varied significantly for a few nutrients. For example, in 1994 and 1996, respectively, 48 percent and 47 percent of the samples were not within the allowable range for vitamin A; 48 percent and 12 percent of the samples were not within the allowable range for vitamin C; and 32 percent and 31 percent of the samples were not within the allowable range for iron.16 These variances are important because consuming too much or too little of certain vitamins and iron may have adverse health consequences. FDA officials cited resource constraints and other priorities as reasons for not updating these studies and told us that FDA has no plans for future studies.

Actions in Response to Labeling Violations Have Generally Decreased or Remained Steady

FDA Warning Letters for Food Labeling Violations Have Remained Steady

FDA has available several tools to ensure that food labeling complies with requirements: (1) issuing warning and untitled letters and holding regulatory meetings and (2) taking enforcement actions—seizures, injunctions, import refusals, and import alerts. However, we found that FDA's efforts have generally declined or held steady.

From fiscal years 2002 through 2007, FDA issued 463 warning letters to firms with serious violations that included food labeling violations—often with other food-safety-related violations—notifying them that enforcement actions might be forthcoming if corrections were not made. The number of warning letters issued annually that included food-labeling-related violations held relatively steady during the period. On the other hand, the number of letters issued for all FDA-regulated products (e.g., food, drugs, and medical devices) decreased by nearly half—from 806 letters in fiscal year 2002 to 434 in fiscal year 2007. However, as we conducted our study, FDA continued to find additional warning letters that had been issued for fiscal years 2002 through 2007. In addition, according to FDA, its Fiscal Year 2007 Enforcement Story reported 471 warning letters for 2007. Thus, the number of food-labeling-related warning letters, as well as total FDA warning letters, may be higher than we report. Figure 3 shows the number of warning letters issued annually for fiscal years 2002 through 2007.

The labeling-related warning letters addressed violations for different product types—including candy, baked goods, seafood, and juice drinks— that were identified through inspections or testing product samples. About 52 percent (241 of 463) of the letters were for dietary supplements. Of the 463 food-labeling-related warning letters, 326 cited specific violations of the misbranding provision of the Federal Food, Drug, and Cosmetic Act; the other 137 letters cited other statutory provisions and regulations.

As shown in table 4, the 326 letters that cited the misbranding provision included references to 677 violations in 15 different categories.

FDA officials explained that they try to focus their oversight efforts on the labeling violations of public health significance and on the types of products with widespread or persistent violations. For example, on October 17, 2005, FDA issued 29 warning letters to manufacturers of cherry juice and other fruit products for unapproved claims related to diseases, and 25 letters on October 12, 2006, to makers of dietary supplement products that had drug claims or unauthorized health claims FDA officials told us that warning letters are an important and very public tool for ensuring compliance with FDA regulations and alerting other companies of practices that are not acceptable. Furthermore, FDA, in accordance with Freedom of Information Act requirements, makes these letters available on its public Web site [17]. However, we found several problems with FDA's public dissemination of warning letters that call into question the accuracy of its numbers. For example, we tested the reliability of this database and found that it was missing over 220 warning letters. When we brought the missing letters to their attention, FDA officials told us they posted them. Although FDA officials assured us that the database was complete and accurate, in February 2008 and later, we found duplicate letters in the database as well as additional letters that had been issued during fiscal years 2006 and 2007.

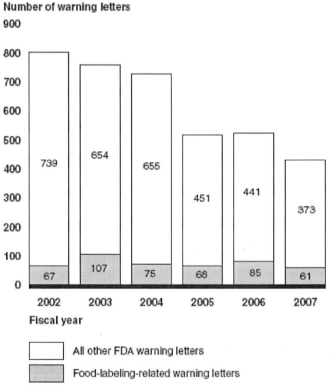

Source: GAO analysis of FDA's online database of warning letters.

Figure 3. FDA Food-Labeling-Related Warning Letters and All Other FDA Warning Letters Issued, Fiscal Years 2002 through 2007.

Table 4. Number of Violations of the Misbranding Provision of the Federal Food, Drug, and Cosmetic Act Cited in 326 FDA Food-Labeling-Related Warning Letters, Fiscal Years 2002 through 2007

Food-labeling-related violation	Number of violations in the 326 letters	Percentage of total violations
Meets the generic finding that the "label is false or misleading in any particular"	163	24.1%
Fails to meet the requirements to bear health and/or nutrient content claims	129	19.1
Fails to declare all of the ingredients by their common or usual name	107	15.8
Does not comply with the format and content requirements for nutrition information	84	12.4
Lacks common or usual name of the food	46	6.8
Lacks name and location of the manufacturer, packer, or distributor	30	4.4
Contains undeclared flavoring, coloring, or chemical preservatives	27	4.0
Bears a drug claim not allowed on a dietary supplement label	25	3.7
Fails to declare accurate weight, quantity, or numerical count	22	3.2
Fails to declare sources of all major food allergens	16	2.4
Does not meet the standard identity indicated on the label	10	1.5
Does not meet standard that information required be prominently placed on the label	9	1.3
Claims, inaccurately, to contain ginseng	5	0.7
Offered for sale under the name of another food	2	0.3
Fails to declare the food is an imitation	2	0.3
Total	677	100%

Source: GAO analysis of FDA warning letters.

Therefore, the number of warning letters posted on FDA's Web site for fiscal years 2002 through 2007 may be different from the number shown in figure 3. In April 2008, FDA officials told us they were continuing to work on the database and to discuss potential process improvements to help ensure that all letters are posted. In fiscal year 2001, FDA had issued nearly twice as many warning letters for all violations than in 2002. FDA officials attributed the decrease in warning letters, in part, to new policies that transferred the approval of warning letters from FDA centers and districts to the Office of Chief Counsel. FDA officials told us that the target turnaround time for issuing a warning letter—the elapsed time between the day officials identify the violation, either through an inspection, laboratory test, or illness outbreak investigation, and the day FDA issues a warning letter—is about 4 months. This is a nearly fourfold increase over the 30-workday target time we reported in February 2005 [18]. A longer lag time to issue a warning letter increases the number of days for which consumers may consume the misbranded food before FDA posts these serious problems on its Web site.

In addition, FDA estimated that it has sent one third as many untitled letters—correspondence citing violations that FDA deems as not warranting a warning letter—as warning letters. We did not assess untitled letters because FDA did not centrally track the letters in a database, nor did it maintain copies centrally until fiscal year 2008. Regarding regulatory meetings, FDA could not tell us how many were held because these meetings are handled exclusively by the district offices and are not centrally tracked. FDA does not receive any information on the extent to which districts are using these meetings and whether the different field offices are using the same criteria for these meetings.

More Serious Enforcement Actions on Labeling Are Generally Limited

FDA has taken few enforcement actions—seizures, injunctions, and import refusals—for food labeling violations and issued a number of labeling- related import alerts. FDA was able to provide us with data on seizures and injunctions for 10 years and on import refusals and import alerts for 6 years.

Seizures: In fiscal years 1998 through 2007, FDA had initiated actions that resulted in court seizures of 21 products in domestic commerce for foodlabeling-related violations. Of the 21 seizures, most were of imported products. Olive oil, dietary supplements, and mushrooms were the most frequently seized products.

Injunctions: According to FDA documents, the courts enjoined two companies in response to possible labeling violations for fiscal years 1998 through 2007 [19]. On February 3, 2006, FDA obtained a consent decree of permanent injunction against Natural Ovens Bakery, Inc., for allegedly introducing misbranded foods, including dietary supplements, and misbranded and unapproved drugs into interstate commerce and for causing foods to become misbranded. According to FDA documents, the injunction was obtained after a

20-year history of noncompliance with FDA regulations, and 3 years after an April 8, 2003, warning letter that FDA's Minneapolis District Office had issued in response to inspections conducted in December 2002, February 2002, and September 2001. The other was a consent decree of permanent injunction, entered in September 2003 against a dietary supplement manufacturer—Hi-Tech Pharmaceuticals, Inc.—for allegedly labeling dietary supplements with drug claims, which violated food labeling requirements and caused FDA to have to regulate the supplements as drugs and, specifically, as unapproved new drugs. FDA considered this injunction to be food-labeling-related.

Import refusals: FDA refused entry to 15,226 imported food product entry lines that had labeling violations from fiscal years 2002 through 2007 [20]. In fiscal year 2002, while FDA examined the fewest labels, it refused entry to the highest percentage of foods; conversely, in fiscal year 2005, FDA examined the greatest number of labels, and refused entry to the lowest percentage of foods over the 6-year period. In addition, over this period, 14,851 products that had labeling violations were released "with comments"—meaning that FDA allowed the shipment with a labeling violation to enter the United States with notice to the importer that subsequent shipments could be refused entry if the violation was not corrected [21]. Releases with comment are intended to cover deficiencies FDA regards as minor, nonhealth-significant. If FDA finds additional imports of one of these products with the same violation 60 or more days after the earlier shipment is released with comments, FDA may consider detention, according to FDA officials (See table 5)

For import refusals, the most frequent labeling violations cited were the lack of required nutrition information (25 percent); the failure to list the common or usual name of each ingredient (18 percent); the failure to accurately state the product's weight, measure, or numerical count (13 percent); and the failure to provide the label in English (12 percent). (See table 6)

Of the nine countries with the greatest value of agricultural, fish, and seafood imports to the United States in fiscal year 2006, Canada was the largest—with a total value of $15.6 billion; Mexico was second with $9.8 billion, followed by China with $4.2 billion. As shown in table 7, during fiscal years 2002 through 2007, Canada also had the most food labels reviewed (45,377) and lowest rate of import refusals (2.6 percent) where a labeling violation was cited, while Australia had the fewest label reviews (697) and the highest rate of import refusals (14.3 percent) where a labeling violation was cited.

Table 5. Number of Imported Food Product Entry Lines Examined for Labeling Compliance, Refused Import, and Released with Comment, Fiscal Years 2002 through 2007

Fiscal year	Product lines examined for labeling compliance		Product lines refused import that had labeling violations		Product lines released with comments that had labeling violations	
	Number		Number	Percentage of total product lines examined	Number	Percentage of total productlines examined
2002	16,275		2,357	14.5%	1,518	9.3%
2003	29,383		2,919	9.9	3,104	10.6
2004	30,598		2,671	8.7	2,657	8.7
2005	38,782		2,498	6.4	2,304	5.9
2006	34,753		2,497	7.2	2,885	8.3
2007	34,215		2,284 ▪	6.7	2,383	7.0
Total	184,006		15,226	8.3%	14,851	8.1%

Source: GAO analysis of FDA Operational and Administrative System Import Support data.

Note: While food labeling was listed as a reason in each import refusal and release with comment, it was not necessarily the only reason, nor was it necessarily the most serious violation.

Table 6. Violations Cited in Food-Labeling-Related Import Refusals, Fiscal Years 2002 through 2007

Food-labeling-related violation	Number of violations	Percentage of total violations
Lacks required nutrition information	6,909	25%
Lacks the common or usual ingredient name	4,840	18
Fails to declare accurate weight, quantity, or numerical count	3,519	13
Lacks information in English	3,348	12
Lacks name and location of the manufacturer, packer, or distributor	1,906	7
Lacks common or usual name of the food	1,576	6
Fails to indicate apparent added coloring	1,022	4
Bears a label that is inconspicuous and unlikely to be read	842	3
Bears false and misleading information	673	2
Bears a label with 1 of 13"other" categories with less than 1 percent of the violations citeda	628	2
Fails to declare apparent color additive Yellow No. 5	552	2
Does not meet FDA's standard of identity	397	1
Fails to declare a chemical preservative	356	1
Fails to declare the trans fat content	222	1
Lacks prominent statement of the percentage of vegetable or fruit juice	217	1
Fails to declare sulfites	174	1
Bears an unauthorized nutrient/health claim	158	1
Total	27,339	100%

Source: GAO analysis of FDA data.aThe "other" category includes 13 types of violations, such as "inaccurately represents fish as catfish" and "fails to declare all major food allergens."

Table 7. Imported Food Products Examined for Labeling Compliance, Products Refused Import, and Products Released With Comment for Fiscal Years 2002 through 2007, for the Top Nine Countries in Value of Agricultural, Fish, and Seafood Imports

Country (value of agricultural, fish, and seafood imports in 2006, in billions)	Examined for labeling compliance	Products			
		Refused import that had labeling violations		Released with comments that had labeling violations	
	Number	Number	Percentage of products examined	Number	Percentage of product sexamined
Canada ($15.6)	45,377	1,174	2.6%	1,538	3.4%
Mexico ($9.8)	25,622	1,964	7.7	830	3.2
Chinaa($4.2)	8,595	655	7.6	991	11.5
Thailand ($3.1)	5,362	253	4.7	489	9.1
Italy ($2.8)	4,891	429	8.8	563	11.5
Indonesia ($2.8)	1,726	156	9.0	173	10.0
Chile ($2.7)	1,136	34	3.0	133	11.7
Australia ($2.6)	697	100	14.3	67	9.6
Brazil ($2.4)	2,321	220	9.5	338	14.6
Total	95,727	4,985	5.2%	5,122	5.4%

Source: GAO analysis of FDA OASIS data and value of imports data for 2006 from USDA's Foreign Agricultural Service.

Note: The country from which a food product was imported is not necessarily the country of origin of the food product. For example, food imported from Canada may have originated in the United Kingdom. In addition, while food labeling was a reason in each of the import refusals and imports released with comment, it was not necessarily the only reason, nor was it necessarily the most serious violation.

[a] The data for China do not include Hong Kong and Macau.

Import alerts: As of January 28, 2008, FDA gave us information on active import alerts for 64 food products that officials characterized as labeling violations. For example, FDA issued import alerts for several different types of biscuits imported from India that did not use the common or usual name for ingredients. Once a product is on the import alert list, FDA does not remove it until the firm appears to have corrected the violation, according to FDA officials. Twenty of the 64 products on import alert were added during fiscal year 2007, and 1 of the remaining 44 had been in effect since April 2000. In technical comments on a draft of this report, FDA indicated that 64 alerts seemed too low and that it may not have provided us with all import alerts for labeling violations. However, FDA did not provide additional information or documentation on those alerts.

FDA Has Collected but Not Analyzed Data on Labeling Violations and Follow-up Actions

FDA does not centrally track or analyze data on potentially serious labeling violations or firms' actions to correct those violations. We repeatedly requested any routine reports on labeling compliance that FDA managers used to help them carry out their program oversight responsibilities. However, according to officials, they do not generate such routine reports due, in part, to resource limitations and to limitations in FDA information systems. For example, over the past decade, FDA has never analyzed the results of the laboratory tests on the accuracy of labeling information (e.g., the Nutrition Facts panel and declared allergens) on domestic and imported foods. An official said they had always wanted to develop computer programs that would identify trends, but did not have the staff to do so. Also, FDA does not routinely analyze and report on trends in labeling violations. As a result, FDA managers do not have important information to inform their decision making on setting priorities for overseeing compliance with labeling requirements and allocating resources for labeling program activities.

Furthermore, FDA does not provide consumers and others with important information on its public Web site to help inform their food purchasing decisions. As we have previously noted, FDA's Web site's posting of warning letters has not been kept current and complete. In addition, although FDA maintains import refusals and warning letters, its Web site does not provide the public with summary information on, and trends in, serious labeling violations by, for example, product type, company, and country.

In addition, from fiscal years 2001 through 2007, FDA documented approximately 2,600 complaints from consumers on food labeling issues in

FACTS—its compliance tracking system. These data included complaints that ingredients—such as allergens—in the food were not listed on the label and may harm consumers' health. However, the data concerning complaints were not entered into FACTS in a way that would facilitate analysis. Specifically, standard terminology was not used and information on complaint resolutions was captured in different data fields. As a result FDA program managers cannot readily use these FACTS data to track the timely and appropriate resolution of consumer labeling complaints.

CFSAN Continues to Maintain Duplicate Recall Database

According to our analysis of FDA's Recall Enterprise System (RE S) database, 409 of the 1,295 food product recalls that firms carried out during fiscal years 2003 through 2007 listed food labeling violations, such as failing to list added chemical preservatives on labels, as a factor. While food labeling was listed as a reason in each of the 409 recalls, it was not necessarily the only reason nor was it necessarily the most serious violation. In addition, almost 57 percent of the labeling-related recalls were for violations that FDA classifies as high risk—that is, posing a reasonable probability of causing serious adverse health consequences or death—such as labels that fail to identify certain allergens in the food, such as tree nuts, that are potentially deadly to individuals who are sensitive to them.

However, CFSAN maintains an unofficial database of food recalls and reported that it was able to identify more labeling-related recalls than we did in using the official RES. In the course of our work, we learned that CFSAN has continued to maintain this unofficial database for food recalls apart from the official RES. In October 2004, we first reported CFSAN's use of this duplicative recall database and the discrepancies between the unofficial data and the official data [22]. At the time, CFSAN program staff told us they used the unofficial database to generate reports for Congress because it contained the most accurate data. We pointed out that keeping the second database raised significant questions about the validity and reliability of the official system. We also pointed out FDA's substantial investment in the RES and the duplication of resources spent maintaining two separate data systems. Although FDA agreed with our recommendation to eliminate the duplicative recall database, it has continued using resources to maintain the second system—resources that could be used on other CFSAN work.

When FDA provided the RES data electronically for our independent analysis, officials told us it was the official source for CFSAN recalls, including the food-labeling-related recalls. We developed criteria for selecting labeling-related recalls on the basis of various labeling terms and sections on food labeling in the Federal Food, Drug, and Cosmetic Act.

FDA agreed that our criteria for identifying labeling-related recalls were valid. In December 2007, FDA provided final fiscal year 2007 data to complete our analysis. Subsequently, in April 2008, as part of our quality assurance procedures, we provided FDA with our list of labeling-related recalls to review for completeness. CFSAN officials informed us in May 2008 that by using their unofficial database, they identified about 250 foodlabeling-related recalls that were not in our list. Of the 250, 171 were in the official system data but were not captured by the criteria we used. Regarding the remaining 79 recalls, we were unable to locate them in the RES data provided to us. In technical comments on a draft of this report, FDA noted that the 79 recalls had coding differences. However, FDA did not provide us with the codes that corresponded to the RES data. We had originally thought that these 79 recalls were missing from the official database and, therefore, were not posted on the FDA public Web site—thus, we drafted a recommendation that FDA post all recalls in a timely manner. However, after FDA commented that the differences could be due to coding, we deleted this recommendation. It appears that the 409 labeling-related recalls we identified may be a minimum number and, thus, may understate the number of recalls with labeling violations. Because we did not receive the unofficial database, we did not independently analyze it or assess its validity and reliability.

FDA REPORTS THAT RESOURCE CONSTRAINTS AND LIMITED AUTHORITY CHALLENGE EFFORTS TOCARRY OUT FOOD-RELATED RESPONSIBILITIES, INCLUDING FOOD LABELING

FDA's Science Board Advisory Committee report, the Commissioner's May 2008 resource needs assessment, and the Food Protection Plan cite challenges to FDA's efforts to carry out food safety and other food-related responsibilities, in part, because its resources have not kept pace with its increasing responsibilities—challenges that directly impact its oversight of labeling requirements. In addition, FDA does not have certain authorities that it reports would allow it to better leverage resources and carry out its food-related missions. These authorities could help FDA administer and enforce the food labeling requirements.

FDA Asserts That Resources Have Not Kept Pace with Growing Responsibilities

According to the Science Board report, the demands on FDA have soared, but resources have not increased in proportion to demand. In the May 2008 resource needs assessment, FDA's Commissioner identified the immediate need for additional resources—for improvements in FDA's science, information technology, and program capabilities—to ensure the safety of FDA-regulated imports and protect the food supply. Likewise, the Food Protection Plan asserts FDA's ever-expanding responsibilities—such as safeguarding the evolving food demands of consumers; overseeing the increasing volume, variety, and sources of imported food; and staying ahead of the emerging threats to food safety and security—and all of the skills, technologies, and initiatives that it is planning to meet these new challenges. However, as we have testified, it is unclear what the total costs will be to fully implement the plan; thus, we continue to have concerns about FDA's lack of specificity on the resource needs [23].

Although FDA received increased funding for new bioterrorism-related responsibilities following September 11, 2001, staffing levels for CFSAN have declined since then and funding (in constant dollars) has stagnated. Between fiscal years 2003 and 2007, the number of FTE employees in CFSAN headquarters dropped about 20 percent, from 950 to 763, and inspection and enforcement staff decreased by about 19 percent, from 2,217 to 1,806 (see app. IV). While funding in nominal dollars increased from $406.8 million in 2003 to $457.1 million in 2007, when adjusted for inflation, funding in the 2 years is nearly the same— $465.7 million and $465.8 million, respectively—in constant 2008 dollars. At the same time, as we have previously noted, the number of FDA-regulated domestic food firms increased more than 10 percent—from about 58,270 in 2003 to about 65,520 in 2007. Also, the number of different imported food product entry lines has tripled in the past 10 years, and imports account for 15 percent of the food supply. Appendix IV provides detailed information on FDA funding and FTEs for each center.

For fiscal years 1999 through 2007, the FTE staff years for the Office of Nutrition, Labeling, and Dietary Supplements reached its highest level in 2002 (88) and its lowest in 2007 (65), according to data provided by FDA finance and other officials. Within the office, funding and staffing for food labeling activities, as estimated by an FDA finance official, have remained fairly steady since fiscal year 2005, the first year for which FDA staff were able to separate resources for labeling-related activities from other Office of Nutrition, Labeling, and Dietary Supplements work (see table 8).

Table 8. Estimated Staffing and Funding for the Office of Nutrition, Labeling, and Dietary Supplements for Fiscal Years 1999 through 2007 and Estimated Staffing and Funding for Food Labeling Related and Other Activities for Fiscal Years 2005 through 2007

Dollars in millions						
	Staffing level (FTEs)			Budget authority		
Fiscal year	Food-labeling-related	Other	Total	Food-labeling-related	Other	Total
1999	a	a	83	a	a	$7.5
2000	a	a	80	a	a	6.9
2001	a	a	73	a	a	6.8
2002	a	a	88	a	a	9.7
2003	a	a	86	a	a	8.6
2004	a	a	83	a	a	10.0
2005	10.0	73.0	83	$1.2	$8.8	10.0
2006	9.0	65.0	74	1.1	7.7	8.8
2007	10.5	54.5	65	1.3	6.9	8.2

Source: FDA CFSAN finance and other officials.

[a]For fiscal years 1999 through 2004, FDA did not separately track the amount of resources used for food-labeling-related activities, according to an FDA finance official.

FDA's Science Board reported on the growing disparity between FDA resources and responsibilities. Noting that the demands on FDA have soared, while resources have not increased proportionately, the committee concluded that the disparity has made it increasingly "impossible" for FDA to maintain its historic public health mission. In the May 2008 resource needs assessment, the FDA Commissioner identified the immediate need for additional staff to enable the agency to affect its food-safety-related goals.

This would benefit administering and enforcing food labeling requirements. In addition, according to FDA officials, the agency generally does not address misleading food labeling because it lacks the resources to conduct the substantive, empirical research on consumer perceptions that it believes it would need to legally demonstrate that a label is misleading, as the agency believes is required by court rulings, such as Pearson v. Shalala, which is discussed in appendix V.

FDA Has Reported That Certain Authorities It Lacks for Food Programs, Including Labeling, Would Help It Leverage Resources and Carry Out Regulatory Responsibilities

The Food Protection Plan identified a number of legislative changes—new authorities FDA recognized were needed, including, among others, the authority to charge user fees for certain reinspections, accredit third-party inspectors for certain reviews, and mandate recalls when voluntary recalls are not effective. FDA has these authorities for certain other products it regulates but not for food labeling activities or most food oversight efforts. In addition, FDA has never used its detention authority under the Bioterrorism Act of 2002 to detain potentially dangerous food because, according to the agency, its other authorities and regulatory tools have been adequate to date to protect public health.

Several FDA centers have the authority to collect user fees for particular activities. For example, FDA's Center for Devices and Radiological Health has the authority to collect and retain user fees from firms for reviewing and approving premarket applications for medical devices. The center uses the fees to offset the costs of reviewing and approving these applications and to increase staffing levels. In its Fiscal Year 2009 Justification of Estimates for Appropriations Committees for FDA, HHS proposed a reinspection user fee on food industry firms that fail to meet important manufacturing and food safety requirements. This fee would cover the full cost of reinspections and the associated follow-up work [24]. We have presented various ways to design user fees to encourage greater efficiency, equity, and revenue adequacy and to reduce the administrative burden on the agency and payers of the fees [25]. For example, the extent to which a program is funded by user fees should generally be guided by who primarily benefits from the program. If a program primarily benefits the general public (e.g., national defense), it should be supported by general revenue, not user fees; if it primarily benefits identifiable users, such as customers of the U.S. Postal Service, it should be funded by fees; and if a program benefits both the general public and users, it should be funded in part by fees and in part by general revenues. The guide may provide useful direction to FDA as it proceeds with its proposed reinspection user fee. (Funding data presented in app. IV also show user fees collected by some FDA centers)

Regarding the authority to accredit qualified third-party inspectors, which the Food Protection Plan states will allow FDA to allocate inspection resources more effectively, FDA plans to use these highly qualified parties to, among other things, carry out certain voluntary reviews in foreign food facilities, where few inspections and label reviews are currently done. As we testified in May 2008,

FDA's Center for Devices and Radiological Health has accredited third-party organizations to conduct voluntary inspections of foreign firms that manufacture medical devices, and these third parties completed six inspections in 4 years [26]. We noted that an incentive for firms to participate included the opportunity to reduce the number of inspections conducted to meet FDA's and other countries' requirements. Disincentives include bearing the cost of the inspections and the potential consequences that could include regulatory action. We further noted that the small number of inspections raised questions about the practicality and effectiveness of using accredited third-party inspectors to quickly help FDA increase the number of foreign firms inspected.

The Food Protection Plan does not describe how FDA expects to design and implement the proposed accredited third-party inspection program to inspect foreign food firms or how this proposal will help it leverage resources. In contrast, USDA uses third-party Agricultural Commodity Meat Graders—contracted for their expertise—to carry out certain reviews in its livestock and meat grading and certification programs.

FDA's Food Protection Plan also asserts that the agency needs mandatory recall authority for food. It has this authority for infant formula and medical devices that present a health hazard. Other agencies, such as the National Highway Traffic Safety Administration and the Consumer Product Safety Commission, use their recall authority to help protect consumers from products that can cause serious injuries, such as unsafe infant car seats. We have previously proposed that Congress consider giving FDA mandatory food recall authority [27].

The Bioterrorism Act of 2002 gave FDA the authority to administratively detain any article of food found during an examination, inspection, or investigation, if it has credible evidence or information indicating that the article of food presents a threat of serious adverse health consequences or death, for labeling and other violations. However, FDA has never used this authority.

According to the agency, its other authorities and regulatory tools, such as its authority to refuse entry of imports under section 801 of the act, have been adequate to date to protect public health. In contrast, USDA has detention authority for meat and poultry products in interstate commerce that its FSIS uses to prevent shipments under its jurisdiction from entering U.S. commerce, if the agency has reason to believe that the food is adulterated or misbranded. USDA reported that, from July through September 2006, its import investigators detained 15 shipments—about 9,500 pounds—of imported meat products.

FDA officials acknowledged that implementing the Food Protection Plan will require additional resources, and that FDA will need to partner with Congress to obtain the additional statutory authorities to transform the safety of the nation's food supply. However, as we testified in May 2008, FDA's congressional outreach strategy is general [28]. When we asked FDA officials if they had a congressional outreach strategy, officials said that they had met with various committees to discuss the Food Protection Plan. When we asked if they had provided draft language to congressional committees on the various authorities, FDA officials explained that they had only provided technical assistance, such as commenting on draft bills, to congressional staff when asked.

KEY STAKEHOLDERS SUGGESTED ACTIONS TO HELP MITIGATE MISLEADING LABELING AND ASSIST CONSUMERS' EFFORTS TO IDENTIFY HEALTHY FOOD

Key stakeholders—officials from health, medical, and consumer organizations in the United States and Europe—advocate a uniform front-of-package symbol to help consumers select healthy food and avoid misleading or confusing labeling. Some U.S. trading partners have implemented voluntary front-of-package nutrition symbols and several U.S. manufacturers and groceries are using front-of-package symbols. In addition, many stakeholders identified or petitioned FDA for other actions that they believe FDA should pursue to avoid misleading labeling and help consumers identify nutritious foods. Some stakeholders noted that taking such actions may require FDA to redirect resources.

Other Countries and Several Key Stakeholders Favor Uniform Front-of-Package Nutrition Symbols

Consumers have reported understanding certain labeling terms, such as "sugar" and "vitamins," and finding benchmarks (such as daily reference values) helpful in comparing products, but they generally found nutrition labeling confusing, especially certain technical and numerical information, according to a recent synthesis of nutrition studies [29]. For example, consumers had difficulty in understanding the role that nutrients played in their diet, and the relationship between sugar and carbohydrates as well as the terms "cholesterol" and "fatty acids." While a few studies suggest that many consumers look at Nutrition Facts panels when they buy food for the first time, some studies suggest that consumers may simply look at the information but not process it further. The National

Academies' Institute of Medicine, which is often called on to advise federal agencies on health issues, reported in 2006 that there is little evidence that the information on food labels has a significant impact overall on eating or food purchasing [30]. The institute had previously recommended that FDA and others increase research on the nutrition label and pointed out that manufacturers' use of nutrition symbols underscores the need to improve strategies for using the food label as an educational tool. In addition, in a November 2007 letter to FDA, the American Medical Association (AMA) stated that there is evidence that consumers have difficulty in making appropriate judgments about which foods are the healthiest.

Several major health and consumer organizations in the United States, as well as in Canada and Europe, advocate mandatory, uniform front-of package nutrition rating systems to help consumers select healthy foods. In the United States, the AMA and the American Heart Association advocate such a system, and the Institute of Medicine's 2006 report recommended that food and beverage companies work with government, scientific, public health, and consumer groups to develop and implement an industrywide system. Furthermore, to help consumers choose more nutritious foods, the scientists with expertise in nutrition and public health who developed the 2005 Dietary Guidelines for Americans expressed concern that consumers did not have a scientifically valid system to show nutrient density on food labels, and recommended that HHS and USDA develop this system. In addition, the Center for Science in the Public Interest petitioned FDA in 2006 to develop a simple, uniform, science-based rating system that could be graphically represented on the front of food packages to give consumers consistent, reliable nutrition information.

Although the European Union does not require nutrition labeling for all foods, it does require it on foods that have health or nutrition claims or that have voluntarily added vitamins or minerals, according to a European Union official. In addition, several countries, including the United Kingdom, the Netherlands, and Sweden, have implemented voluntary, front-of-package nutrition labeling systems, while Canada is proposing research on how such systems influence food purchases, among other things, and consulting stakeholders. The European Commission has proposed a mandatory, front-of-package labeling system.

Figure 4 shows the front-of-package nutrition symbols for systems in the United Kingdom, the Netherlands, and Sweden, which help consumers in those countries identify healthy foods Consumers and health organizations in many countries have a heightened interest in the benefits of choosing healthy foods, including several that have implemented (see figure 4) or are considering front-of-package nutrition labeling systems.

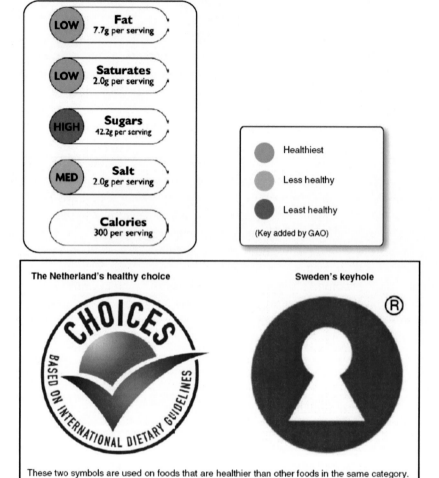

An example of a United Kingdom traffic light

LOW	**Fat** 7.7g per serving
LOW	**Saturates** 2.0g per serving
HIGH	**Sugars** 42.2g per serving
MED	**Salt** 2.0g per serving
	Calories 300 per serving

Healthiest

Less healthy

Least healthy

(Key added by GAO)

The Netherland's healthy choice

Sweden's keyhole

These two symbols are used on foods that are healthier than other foods in the same category.

Sources: Government officials from the United Kingdom, the Netherlands, and Sweden.

Figure 4. Selected Front-of-Package Symbols Used in Other CountriesConsumers.

For example:

- *The United Kingdom*: The Food Standards Agency implemented a voluntary front-of-package traffic light symbol to help consumers distinguish between the healthiest choices (green light), less-healthy choices (amber light), and least healthy choices (red light) with respect to fat, saturated fat, salt, sugars, and usually calories, as well. Officials report that preliminary sales data suggest that this system is influencing consumers' purchases toward healthier products. In addition, manufacturers are developing new products and reformulating less-healthy products so that their foods may move into the amber or green light category, according to U.K. officials. The United Kingdom's National Heart Forum (an alliance of 50 heart health organizations) has endorsed the traffic light system.

- *The Netherlands:* The Netherlands uses a voluntary front-of-package "healthy choice" symbol, which was developed by the food industry and endorsed by the Ministry of Health. According to a Ministry official, standards for applying the symbol vary by food category, taking into account the characteristics of each category—for example, fiber is included in the criteria for bread products. A foundation was established—the Choices International Foundation—to introduce the symbol to other countries. The qualifying criteria for using the symbol will be reevaluated every 2 years by an independent scientific committee, according to the official.

- *Sweden:* The National Food Administration uses a voluntary front-of-`package keyhole logo to identify the healthiest foods within particular food categories. Products that carry the symbol are lower in fats, sugars, and sodium and contain more fiber than other foods within the same category. According to agency officials, the introduction of the keyhole logo resulted in the development of healthier products and the continuous reformulation of existing products.

- *Canada:* The House of Commons' Committee on Health's 2007 report, Healthy Weights For Healthy Kids, recommended that the country's health agency—Health Canada—phase in a mandatory, standard, simple, front-of-package labeling requirement for prepackaged food, starting with foods advertised primarily to children. In addition, the Chronic Disease Prevention Alliance of Canada supports this recommendation. As of April 2008, Health Canada commented that it is taking several steps, including consulting with stakeholders and proposing consumer research on, among other things, front-of-package symbols.

- *European Union:* The European Commission has proposed legislation that would require prepackaged food to display information on calories, fat, saturated fat, carbohydrates, sugars, and salt on package fronts, according to documents released by the commission [31]. A commission official told us that member states would still be able to promote additional national front-of-package labeling systems if they comply with requirements of the proposed legislation. The European Union's Commissioner for Health stated that food labels can have a huge influence on consumers' purchasing decisions, and confusing, overloaded, or misleading labels can be a hindrance to consumers. The European Heart Network (an alliance of 30 heart health organizations in 26 countries) and the European Consumers' Organization also support mandatory front-of-package labeling.

In the United States, health and consumer associations have developed nutrition symbols to help consumers. For example, the American Heart Association developed the heart-check logo to help consumers identify heart-healthy foods. Currently, over 800 products from over 100 companies use the logo, and one major line of foods was developed with the heart- check criteria as a key driver, according to the association. While most companies reformulate products before applying for the logo certification, the association also works with companies on 20 to 40 products a year to help them meet its criteria. In addition, the Whole Grains Council, a nonprofit consumer group working to increase consumption of whole grains, developed the Whole Grain Stamp to identify products with at least a half serving of whole grains, with the grams of whole grain specified. A "100%" banner can be placed on the stamps when all of the grain is whole grain. The stamps have been used on over 1,700 products from 180 companies in the United States, Canada, and the United Kingdom.

In addition, manufacturers have developed numerous symbols to market their foods to health-conscious consumers, and supermarkets have used symbols to help consumers identify healthier foods. At a September 2007 FDA public hearing on front-of-package and other nutrition symbols several manufacturers and supermarket chains reported increased sales and reformulations associated with their use of nutrition symbols. For example, Kraft has reported that the more than 500 products carrying its Sensible Solution symbol accounted for a sizable portion of its overall revenue growth. Hannaford, a northeastern supermarket chain, reported that it improved the nutrient quality of its store brand products before introducing its symbol for nutrition quality that it calls Guiding Stars, which is based on mathematical formulas giving a weighted value to many nutrients. Hannaford also reported increased sales for products with stars.

According to the Institute of Medicine, however, the consistency, accuracy, and effectiveness of the proprietary graphics currently in use have not been evaluated or empirically validated, and they may fall short of their potential as guides to more nutritious choices. Many stakeholders also share a concern about the proliferation of such graphics. FDA officials told us that the agency assigned an individual part time to focus on research on nutrition symbols. In comments, FDA told us it has completed one study. In addition, FDA plans to issue a summary of the 2007 public hearing and to identify gaps in the information that stakeholders provided during or after the hearing, at the request of FDA.

The Grocery Manufacturers/Food Products Association opposes mandatory front-of-package nutrition symbols and maintains that nutrition symbols should continue to be voluntary because the industry's use of symbols to communicate nutrition information is truthful, not misleading, and consistent with FDA's clear regulations for making representations about nutrition. According to the association, in recent years, many food companies have reformulated thousands of food products to improve their nutrient profiles, and many manufacturers are using symbols and related graphic designs on labels to supplement the Nutrition Facts panel. In addition, the Keystone Center, an industry-funded nonprofit organization, has held discussions to determine whether it should develop a voluntary front-of-package system. In 2007, the center convened a group of experts from industry, government, consumer, and academic organizations to study the various systems used in the United States. As of July 2008, this group had not released information on the status of its effort. According to FDA officials, FDA acts as an observer in this group. However, FDA has not yet collaborated with the relevant federal agencies and stakeholders with nutrition expertise to evaluate labeling approaches and options.

Stakeholders Suggested Other Actions That FDA Should Take to Help Consumers Identify Healthy Foods

Several medical, health, and consumer association stakeholders suggested FDA actions that they believe would mitigate misleading and confusing labeling. While some stakeholders noted that these actions may require FDA to redirect resources, they also believe such actions would help consumers identify healthy foods.

- *Eliminate qualified health claims*: Stakeholders, such as the AMA, have suggested that FDA eliminate the use of qualified health claims on food labels because consumers cannot distinguish among the four levels of scientific support that FDA uses—significant scientific agreement, scientific evidence that is not conclusive, limited scientific evidence that is not conclusive, and very little scientific and preliminary evidence. According to the stakeholders, these claims confuse or mislead consumers and may encourage the consumption of foods with little or no health benefits. This view was supported by findings from 2005 and 2007 FDA studies [32]. In commenting on a draft of this report, FDA questioned whether it had the authority to eliminate the use of such claims. See appendix V for more information on FDA's administration of health claims.

- *Establish criteria for characterizing the amount of whole grains in food*: The use of the term "whole grain" increased in popularity after the 2005 Dietary Guidelines underscored the importance of these foods in the American diet. Some studies suggest that consumers, as well as dieticians and other nutrition experts, cannot accurately identify which foods are primarily whole grain. In 2004, General Mills, Inc., petitioned FDA to establish criteria for the phrases "excellent source of whole grains," "good source of whole grains," and "made with whole grains" to help prevent false or misleading labeling of grain products. FDA denied the petition, but it acknowledged the need for action and stated that claims such as "good source" have been used only with regard to nutrients—not foods—and that FDA needs to consider how to classify different kinds of statements and whether public comments are needed. In 2006, FDA developed draft guidance that identified what foods it considered "whole grain."[33] FDA officials stated that they expect to continue work on this issue when they can hire additional staff.

- *Prohibit foods that contain substantial amounts of saturated fat from being labeled as "trans fat free"*: FDA has not objected to products being labeled as "trans fat free" that have less than 0.5 grams of trans fat per serving, and does not restrict the amount of saturated fat in "trans fat free" foods. However, as stakeholders pointed out, saturated fat, like trans fat, raises low density lipoprotein (LDL or "bad cholesterol") levels in the blood, increasing the risk of heart disease. Initially, FDA proposed limiting "trans fat free" labeling to foods with less than 0.5 grams of saturated fat, but FDA later stated that insufficient scientific information existed to support whether 0.5 was the appropriate level. FDA is evaluating available research to determine how to best address the issue.

- *Require the labels of foods commonly consumed in one sitting to show total calories, fat, and other nutrition information*: Several health and consumer stakeholders believe consumers may be misled by Nutrition Facts panels for foods, such as large sodas, candy bars, muffins, and other foods, that are normally consumed in one sitting, but are labeled as two or more servings. In 2005, the Institute of Medicine recommended that

FDA revise requirements so that foods typically consumed in one sitting prominently display the total calorie content of the product as well as the standard per-serving format [34]. Industry- sponsored research found that the participants in four focus groups generally favored the listing of nutrients for the whole container, although some want nutrients listed for both the full container and per serving. In April 2005, FDA published an advance notice of proposed rulemaking requesting comments on this issue. In 2008, FDA noted that it needed to review the comments submitted in response to the 2005 notice, and to coordinate this area with its plans to revise the daily intake reference values (used to establish the daily values for the Nutrition Facts panel) described in a 2007 advance notice of proposed rulemaking. The Grocery Manufacturers/Food Products Association opposes requiring nutrition information for the entire contents of the package on the food label, noting that nutrition information for the entire package would give consumers "permission" or "encouragement" to eat the entire package.

- *Clarify the definition of "natural" as it applies to food*: The Sugar Association has petitioned, with the support of the Center for Science in the Public Interest and others, that FDA define the term "natural" on the basis of USDA's definition, as articulated in its Foods Standards and Labeling Policy Book. USDA policy defines "natural" to permit only minimal processing, including roasting, drying, and fermenting, to preserve or make food edible. Under this USDA policy, foods that go through certain processes, such as chemical bleaching, that fundamentally alter the raw product, are not considered "natural." Both groups assert that FDA allows manufacturers to label products as "100% natural" even if they contain highly processed ingredients, citing partially hydrogenated oils and high fructose corn syrup. However, the Corn Refiners Association believes that USDA and FDA should have different definitions of "natural" because, among other things, the two agencies regulate fundamentally different products—USDA-regulated meat and poultry products are understood to be less processed than FDA-regulated foods. FDA acknowledged in 1993 that clarifying the definition of "natural" would abate some of the complaints that the term's use is misleading. More recently, FDA noted that it lacks resources to undertake a rulemaking to revisit the definition.

CONCLUSIONS

With its current approach to oversight and enforcement, FDA cannot be assured that food firms are complying with labeling requirements. In light of the resource constraints and many responsibilities that FDA has reported, it is especially important that FDA start by making better use of the tools and data it has available. However, FDA's use of warning letters and enforcement actions have at best held steady, despite increased responsibilities. FDA is not using the information that it has to inform managers' decisions on setting priorities and allocating resources. FDA does not maintain in an accessible format, or analyze in routine reports, information it has on such areas as labeling violations discovered during inspections, the results of tests on the accuracy of labels, warning letters, recalls, and import refusals. Moreover, although information on whether and how labeling violations are addressed is critical for effectively overseeing the labeling program. FDA does not (1) centrally maintain information on regulatory meetings and (2) know whether field offices are applying the same criteria for meetings and whether meetings are effective While FDA posts information for the public on its Web site—such as warning letters, import refusals, and import alerts—it does not ensure that the information is complete and posted promptly. As a result, the public may not have the information needed about products in violation of the law to inform their purchase decisions. Furthermore, CFSAN has continued to expend resources maintaining a duplicative data system for food-related recalls, which it agreed to eliminate in 2004. We reiterate our prior recommendation that FDA should eliminate this system.

Going forward, to better administer and enforce labeling requirements, FDA has begun to pursue several authorities that are available to other centers within FDA and other regulatory agencies. In particular, CFSAN does not have the authority to charge user fees, accredit third-party inspectors, or require recalls for most food. As a result, CFSAN is not as well positioned as other programs that have these authorities to carry out its responsibilities. FDA's Food Protection Plan recognized the need for additional resources and new authorities, to ensure the safety of the Nation's food supply. However, as FDA proceeds in seeking new authorities it will need to ensure that any it chooses to pursue are designed and implemented efficiently and appropriately and, in particular, that any user fees it develops are well-designed and based on best practices and sound criteria, such as that specified in GAO's Federal User Fees: A Design Guide.35 In addition, any FDA program for accrediting third parties would likely benefit from lessons learned in another FDA-accredited third-party program. Moreover, as we have previously testified, while FDA's plan is a good first step, it does not contain a clear description of resources and strategies. Congress will need those details to assess the likelihood of the plan's success.

Finally, the many issues stakeholders raised about label information that they believe confuse consumers compete for FDA's attention and resources. Nonetheless, FDA has information on the approaches that U.S. industry and other countries are taking to give consumers simplified nutrition information at a glance with front-of-package symbols. However, given FDA's competing priorities and its minimal progress in addressing misleading labeling thus far, collaboration with other federal entities and stakeholders could afford an opportunity for FDA to better leverage resources to pursue front-of-package labeling or other initiatives for minimizing consumer confusion.

RECOMMENDATIONS FOR EXECUTIVE ACTION

We recommend that the Commissioner, FDA, take the following seven actions:

Ensure that labeling office managers have the information they need to oversee compliance with food labeling statutes and regulations by

- maintaining, in a searchable format, data on food labeling violations, including the type of violation and information about corrective actions taken or, if no action was taken, the reason why;
- analyzing violation data in routine management reports; and
- tracking regulatory meetings related to food labeling violations and analyzing whether regulatory meetings are an effective use of resources.

Ensure that the public has timely access to information on food labeling violations that may have serious health consequences by requiring all of the centers and offices to post on FDA's public Web site, within a specified time frame, key information, such as all warning letters; statistics on serious enforcement actions (e.g., import refusals) by country, type of food, and the problem found (e.g., undeclared allergen); and information (e.g., product identification and exposure symptoms) on violations that FDA classifies as serious.

Better leverage resources to carry out food safety and other regulatory responsibilities, including administering and enforcing labeling requirements, by:

- providing Congress with specific, detailed information on the new statutory authorities identified in the Food Protection Plan, such as the authority to charge user fees, accredit third-party inspectors, and mandate food recalls, with specific information on how these authorities would help achieve its mission;
- posting on FDA's public Web site periodic updates of the status of implementation of the Food Protection Plan, including goals achieved and time frames for completing the remaining work; and collaborating with other federal agencies and stakeholders experienced in nutrition and health issues, to evaluate labeling approaches and options for developing a simplified, empirically valid system that conveys overall nutritional quality to mitigate labels that are misleading to consumers.

AGENCY COMMENTS AND OUR EVALUATION

We provided a draft of this report to HHS for review and comment. In written comments, FDA stated that the report raised some important issues regarding its regulation of food labeling. FDA did not dispute the report's data, analyses, or specific findings. It commented, however, that the report inappropriately references food labeling as part of its food safety mission, although it acknowledges that there may be some aspects of food labeling that can affect the safe use of food. That notwithstanding, FDA directs investigators to review at least three labels during food safety inspections. Moreover, food labeling responsibilities are part of FDA's statutory mission, and the Federal Food, Drug, and Cosmetics Act and FDA's regulations set out FDA's labeling responsibilities. FDA also stated that within its overall public health mission, it has a multitude of competing priorities. We acknowledged FDA's competing priorities in the report's conclusions and framed the recommendations so as to help manage these competing priorities by better leveraging resources and using available tools and data for risk-based decisions.

Regarding our first three recommendations for ensuring that managers have the information they need to oversee compliance with food labeling statutes and regulations—by (1) maintaining data on labeling violations and the corrective actions taken, in a searchable format, (2) analyzing that data in routine management reports, and (3) tracking regulatory meetings on labeling violations to assess whether they are an effective use of resources—FDA agreed that being able to track any and all information that would allow investigators to better do their jobs would be useful to the agency. However, FDA stated that data collection requires time and effort and it is important to make sure that data entry does not become so burdensome that it takes away from other investigative work. FDA did not commit to taking any actions in response to these recommendations. We maintain that FDA cannot make risk-based decisions, such as allocating resources efficiently and effectively, without careful analysis of this type of data on its regulatory programs—FDA's systems already maintain substantial data on food labeling and related violations. Analyzing these data for routine reports could help inform labeling managers' decisions and help them target labeling resources. We stand by these recommendations.

With respect to our recommendation for ensuring the public has timely access to information on labeling violations that may have serious health consequences—that FDA require centers and offices to post key information (e.g., warning letters or import refusals) on FDA's public Web site and specify time frames for doing so—FDA commented that it already posts and maintains much of this information, and that it would keep the information as up to date as possible, given resource and time limitations. However, as we discuss in this report, FDA's target time for issuing warning letters and posting them is 4 months after violations are found. Providing information that is complete and timely can help the public avoid potentially dangerous food and make healthy food purchase decisions. The draft we sent to FDA for comment recommended that FDA post all recalls to its public Web site in a timely manner. We eliminated recalls from this recommendation because, in technical comments, FDA told us that the recalls in CFSAN's unofficial database that we thought were missing from RES were the result of coding differences. We stand by this recommendation as amended.

Our final three recommendations are aimed at better leveraging resources. Two are aimed at helping FDA keep the Food Protection Plan on track by (1) providing specific, detailed information to Congress on how the new authorities in the Food Protection Plan will help FDA achieve its mission and (2) posting periodic updates on the status and time frames for implementing the plan on FDA's public Web site. FDA stated that the plan was designed to address food safety and defense concerns, although some of the actions presented in it may have some bearing on food labeling issues. It was not our intent to suggest that the plan's primary focus was on food labeling; we have clarified this in the report. Nonetheless, in this report and in recent testimonies, we have expressed our concerns that FDA has not given Congress sufficient, detailed information on how it will implement the plan and use the new authorities—information Congress needs to support the initiatives. Furthermore, updates can reassure the public of FDA's progress. FDA did not explicitly address what action, if any, it would take in response to these two recommendations. With respect to our last recommendation—that FDA collaborate with other federal agencies and stakeholders on evaluating options for developing a simplified, empirically valid system for conveying overall nutritional quality to help consumers—FDA agreed with the need to evaluate the communication effects of nutrition symbols and presented a research agenda. Because the agenda appears to be ambitious given FDA's limited resources, our recommendation will continue to encourage FDA to collaborate with other federal agencies and stakeholders who may be able to contribute resources, as it evaluates options to develop a simple, valid system to communicate nutritional quality FDA's written comments and our detailed evaluation appear in appendix VI. FDA also provided technical comments, which we incorporated throughout the report, as appropriate.

As agreed with your office, unless you publicly announce the contents of the report earlier, we plan no further distribution of it until 30 days from the date of this report. At that time, we will send copies of the report to the appropriate congressional committees, the Secretary of Health and Human Services, the Commissioner of the Food and Drug Administration, and other interested parties. We will also make copies available to others upon request. In addition, the report will be available at no charge on the GAO Web site at http://www.gao.gov.

If you or members of your staff have any questions about this report, please contact me at (202) 512-3841 or shamesl@gao.gov. Contact points for our Offices of Congressional Relations and Public Affairs may be found on the last page of this report. GAO staff who made key contributions to this report are listed in appendix VII.

Sincerely yours,

Lisa Shames
Director, Natural Resources and Environment

APPENDIX I
OBJECTIVES, SCOPE, AND METHODOLOGY

This report examines (1) the Food and Drug Administration's (FDA) efforts to ensure that domestic and imported foods comply with food labeling requirements, including those prohibiting false or misleading labeling; (2) the challenges FDA faces in its efforts to administer and enforce food labeling requirements; and (3) the actions that stakeholders from health, medical, and consumer organizations believe are needed to mitigate the effects of food labeling practices they consider misleading and to help consumers identify healthy food.

For the purposes of this report, our definition of "food" includes conventional food, dietary supplements, infant formula, and medical food, [1] but not animal feed, which the Federal Food, Drug, and Cosmetic Act includes in its definition of food. We did not determine whether any particular food labeling was false or misleading. We also did not evaluate how efficiently FDA used its resources or the impact of changing priorities; nor did we compare FDA resource trends with other federal agencies' resource trends. Regarding data for labeling-related oversight, we analyzed the food firms inspected for 7 fiscal years (2001 through 2007); nutrient labeling samples for 7 fiscal years (2000 through 2006); warning letters and enforcement actions related to imports for 6 fiscal years (2002 through 2007); and seizures and injunctions for 10 fiscal years (1998 through 2007)—the periods for which reliable and comparable FDA data were available. Funding and staffing data for FDA, the Center for Food Safety and Applied Nutrition (CFSAN), and the Office of Regulatory Affairs (ORA) were available for 10 fiscal years (1998 through 2007). For the Office of Nutrition, Labeling, and Dietary Supplements, which began maintaining comparable data in 1999, we report funding and staffing for 9 fiscal years (1999 through 2007). Unless otherwise stated, data are presented by federal fiscal year.

To determine FDA's efforts to ensure that domestic and imported foods comply with food labeling statutes and regulations, including those related to false or misleading labeling, we analyzed FDA's and CFSAN's plans and reports, guidance and regulations related to food labeling, and policies and actions taken in response to petitions and complaints over the last 6 years We also analyzed data from the Field Accomplishments and Compliance Tracking System (FACTS) and Operational and Administrative System for Import Support (OASIS) on domestic, foreign, and import inspections conducted by FDA, along with domestic inspections conducted by states under contract with FDA. To determine the number of warning letters issued by FDA, we worked with FDA's Freedom of

Information Office and ORA to address several problems we found during the course of our review regarding the online database of warning letters. After addressing those problems, we then searched that database for warning letters that were related to food labeling and characterized each letter according to the product and the violations cited. We also searched FDA's Recall Enterprise System (RE S) for recalls identified with food labeling violations as one of the reasons for the recall. Regarding violations of Nutrition Facts panel regulations, we analyzed data from FACTS for domestic and imported food, and also analyzed studies conducted on the accuracy of nutrient labeling. We analyzed data from this system on consumer complaints to determine the extent to which they were tracked.

Finally, we also analyzed data from OASIS on food labeling violations for imported food and collected information on seizures and injunctions focused on food labeling violations.

To identify challenges, we analyzed funding and staffing data for FDA, CFSAN, ORA, and the Office of Nutrition Labeling and Dietary Supplements and reviewed FDA oversight and enforcement authorities, and court rulings regarding FDA labeling.

For comparison, we examined some of the same information for the U.S. Department of Agriculture's Food Safety and Inspection Service and the Federal Trade Commission, which also oversee and enforce requirements related to food labeling, such as those prohibiting false or misleading information about food.

We assessed the reliability of the data from FACTS and OASIS that we used in this report and found them to be sufficiently reliable for these purposes. To assess the reliability of these data, we (1) performed electronic testing for obvious errors in accuracy and completeness, (2) reviewed related documentation, and (3) worked closely with agency officials to identify any data problems.

In addition, we assessed the reliability of the data from the RES. FDA recently informed us that CFSAN has continued to use an unofficial database that it agreed to eliminate in 2004, which contains additional information on recalls that would potentially fit our criteria for analysis. Despite any limitations of the RES, we believe these data to be sufficiently reliable to indicate a minimum number of recalls for the time period we reported.

To determine stakeholders' views, we analyzed petitions, public responses to petitions, and ideas presented during FDA's November 2007 public labeling meetings. We discussed these and other suggestions with health and medical associations, including the American Cancer Society, American Diabetic Association, American Heart Association, American Dietetic Association, American Medical Association, and National Academies' Institute of Medicine;

the Center for Science in the Public Interest; the Grocery Manufacturers/Food Products Association; the Association of Food and Drug Officials; and selected states (California, Connecticut, Florida, New York, Texas, and Wisconsin) that the Association of Food and Drug Officials and others groups identified as being active in food labeling issues. In addition, we contacted officials of health or related departments in Canada, the United Kingdom, Sweden, the Netherlands, and the European Commission to collect information on their use or plans for use of nutrition symbols. We did not independently verify the statements of foreign law.

We also analyzed consumer studies conducted by FDA, industry, and others to identify whether the findings supported or failed to support stakeholders' views. These studies were identified by health, consumer, and industry experts and through literature searches. For the data we included in our report, we obtained frequency counts, survey instruments, and other documents, to review the wording of questions, sampling, mode of administration, research strategies, and the effects of sponsorship. We used only data that we judged to be reliable and valid.

We conducted this performance audit from January 2007 through September 2008 in accordance with generally accepted government auditing standards. Those standards require that we plan and perform the audit to obtain sufficient, appropriate evidence to provide a reasonable basis for our findings and conclusions based on our audit objectives. We believe that the evidence obtained provides a reasonable basis for our findings and conclusions based on our audit objectives.

APPENDIX II
FDA-REGULATED AND -INSPECTED DOMESTIC AND FOREIGN FOOD FIRMS, FISCAL YEARS 2001 THROUGH 2007

Nearly half of the domestic firms that are subject to FDA regulation are food firms—manufacturers, processors, and other food businesses. Table 9 presents the number and percentage of domestic food firms that are subject to FDA's food regulations and the total number of domestic firms in all industries (e.g., pharmaceuticals and medical devices) that are subject to FDA regulation, for fiscal years 2001 through 2007.

Regarding firms inspected under all FDA regulatory programs, food-related firms have accounted for between 15 percent and 30 percent of foreign firms inspected and between 45 percent and 56 percent of domestic firms inspected. Table 10 presents the number and percentage of foreign and domestic food-related firms inspected and the total number of FDA- regulated firms inspected, for fiscal years 2001 through 2007, by FDA and states under contract with FDA.

Table 9. Domestic Food Firms and Total Domestic Firms under FDA's Jurisdiction, by Fiscal Year

Fiscal year	Domestic food firms	Total domestic firms	Percentage of totaldomestic firms
2001	51,020	114,696	44.5%
2002	58,593	120,403	48.7
2003	58,268	120,403	48.4
2004	59,305	123,892	47.9
2005	61,930	127,887	48.4
2006	62,929	136,129	46.2
2007	65,520	139,176	47.1

Source: GAO analysis of FDA data.

Note: Food firm data were calculated by adding together food, vitamin, and color additive firms. Some firms may do business in multiple industries; as a result, there may be double-counting.

Table 10. Firms Inspected by FDA and States under Contract with FDA, Fiscal Years 2001 through 2007

Fiscal year	Foreign firms inspected by FDA			Domestic firms inspected by FDA			Domestic firms inspected under contracts with states			Total firms inspected[a]		
	Food firms	Total firms	Food firms as a percentage of total firms	Food firms	Total firms	Food firms as a percentage of total firms	Food firms	Total firms	Food firms as a percentage of total firms	Food firms	Total firms	Food firms as a percentage of total firms
2001	211	892	23.7%	8,922	16,006	55.7%	6,688	16,875	39.6%	14,932	32,733	45.6%
2002	169	791	21.4	8,175	16,428	49.8	6,979	19,885	35.1	14,877	36,216	41.1
2003	148	757	19.6	10,507	20,027	52.5	7,674	19,710	38.9	17,658	39,429	44.8
2004	153	932	16.4	10,370	19,264	53.8	8,173	20,916	39.1	18,172	40,173	45.2
2005	132	844	15.6	8,258	17,489	47.2	8,849	21,493	41.2	16,809	38,924	43.2
2006	125	788	15.9	7,071	15,485	45.7	8,447	23,054	36.6	15,332	38,558	39.8
2007	96	327	29.1	6,106	13,395	45.6	8,692	22,967	37.8	14,661	36,199	40.5

Source: GAO analysis of FDA data.

[a]Since this table reflects the number of firms inspected, not the number of inspections, "total firms inspected" tallies the unique firms inspected in a fiscal year. Firms inspected by both FDA and a state under contract with FDA are counted in each of those individual totals, but only once in "total firms inspected." Firms were counted in each fiscal year they were inspected.

APPENDIX III. FDA INSPECTIONS OF FOOD FIRMS IN FOREIGN COUNTRIES, FISCAL YEARS 2001 THROUGH 2007

Country	Number of FDA inspections of foreign food firms, by fiscal year							
	2001	2002	2003	2004	2005	2006	2007	Total
Mexico	17	15	8	15	7	16	26	104
Ecuador	8		11	24		11	10	64
Chile	13		15	6	7	11		52
Peru	13			18	1	9	9	50
Brazil		12	6	7	21			46
Thailand	4	10		10		22		46
Canada	13		13	1		7	4	38
China		9	2	6	16			33
Taiwan	9	7		9		7		32
Argentina	7	5					19	31
India	6		10		7	7		30
South Korea	14			1	7		6	28
Australia	12		6			9		27
Costa Rica		11		4	5	7		27
Vietnam		9		10	8			27
Honduras	9	8			7			24
Fiji			8				13	21
Singapore	10			8				18
Estonia	8			8				16
Guatemala		10			6			16
South Africa	5		11					16
Germany	5	4	4			1	1	15
Nicaragua		8				7		15
El Salvador			8		6			14
Jamaica	2	6		3		3		14
Latvia	7			7				14
Uruguay		14						14
Venezuela	7				7			14
Italy	4		8				1	13
Morocco	13							13
New Zealand		6				7		13
Poland		13						13

Country	Number of FDA inspections of foreign food firms, by fiscal year							
	2001	2002	2003	2004	2005	2006	2007	Total
Norway				5			6	11
France		1	9					10
Romania			10					10
Surinam					10			10
Iceland		9						9
Malaysia					9			9
Bulgaria	8							8
Colombia					8			8
Hong Kong	8							8
Cyprus				7				7
Panama			7					7
Trinidad and Tobago		7						7
The United Kingdom	1	1	2			1	1	6
Turkey	5							5
Spain			4					4
Belgium		2	1					3
Greece	3							3
Hungary				3				3
Finland			2					2
Haiti			1	1				2
Japan			2					2
The Netherlands		2						2
Total	211	169	148	153	132	125	96	1,034

Source: GAO analsysis of FDA data.

APPENDIX IV. FUNDING AND STAFFING INFORMATION BY FDA MISSION, FISCAL YEARS 1998 THROUGH 2007

Dollars in millions

	1998 FTE	1998 $	1999 FTE	1999 $	2000 FTE	2000 $	2001 FTE	2001 $
Budget authority, by FDA mission								
Foods (mission includes cosmetics)	**2,239**	**$206.2**	**2,339**	**$235.2**	**2,386**	**$279.7**	**2,445**	**$287.5**
Center for Food Safety and Nutrition	784	87.8	784	99.9	830	124.6	879	125.9
Office of Regulatory Affairs	1,455	118.5	1,555	135.3	1,556	155.1	1,566	161.6
Human Drugs	**1,959**	**199.6**	**1,846**	**200.4**	**1,838**	**215.5**	**1,824**	**218.5**
Center for Drug Evaluation and Research	1,241	142.2	1,130	139.7	1,168	152.2	1,140	151.5
Office of Regulatory Affairs	718	57.4	716	60.7	670	63.3	684	67.0
Biologics	**841**	**95.5**	**791**	**95.0**	**780**	**106.1**	**786**	**108.3**
Center for Biologics Evaluation and Research	619	77.7	592	77.8	576	87.5	561	86.2
Office of Regulatory Affairs	222	17.8	199	17.2	204	18.6	225	22.1
Animal Drugs andF eeds	**391**	**41.4**	**393**	**43.3**	**406**	**49.6**	**442**	**64.1**
Center for Veterinary Medicine	251	28.6	254	30.7	271	36.5	290	48.4
Office of Regulatory Affairs	140	12.7	139	12.6	135	13.1	152	15.6
Devices and Radiological Products	**1,507**	**144.3**	**1,432**	**145.8**	**1,426**	**157.7**	**1,428**	**165.3**
Center for Devices and Radiological Health	1,003	103.8	966	105.6	988	116.0	986	122.0
Office of Regulatory Affairs	504	40.5	466	40.2	438	41.6	442	43.3
National Center for Toxicological Research	**218**	**32.2**	**223**	**32.1**	**217**	**36.5**	**206**	**36.2**
Rent andF acilities[a]	**0**	**100.0**	**0**	**124.9**	**0**	**130.7**	**0**	**151.4**
Other[b]	**928**	**112.7**	**827**	**108.6**	**675**	**72.3**	**674**	**68.0**
Subtotal 8	,083	$931.9	7,851	$985.3	7,728	$1,048.1	7,805	$1,099.3
User fees, byF DA mission								
Foods (mission includes cosmetics)	**0**	**$0**	**0**	**$0**	**0**	**$0**	**0**	**$0**
Center for Food Safety and Nutrition	0	0	0	0	0	0	0	0
Office of Regulatory Affairs	0	0	0	0	0	0	0	0
Human Drugs	**467**	**84.6**	**610**	**77.9**	**671**	**95.7**	**711**	**104.0**
Center for Drug Evaluation and Research	398	78.7	551	71.8	604	88.2	644	97.0
Office of Regulatory Affairs	69	5.9	59	6.1	67	7.5	67	7.0
Biologics	**192**	**26.6**	**198**	**29.3**	**211**	**34.6**	**255**	**38.9**
Center for Biologics Evaluation and Research	187	26.1	195	29.0	204	33.8	248	36.2
Office of Regulatory Affairs	5	0.5	3	0.3	7	0.8	7	2.7
Animal Drugs andF eeds	**0**	**0**	**0**	**0**	**0**	**0**	**0**	**0**
Center for Veterinary Medicine	0	0	0	0	0	0	0	0
Office of Regulatory Affairs	0	0	0	0	0	0	0	0
Devices and Radiological Products	**51**	**13.8**	**48**	**13.2**	**46**	**12.6**	**45**	**12.3**

2002 FTE	$	2003 FTE	$	2004 FTE	$	2005 FTE	$	2006 FTE	$	2007 FTE	$
2,734	$393.3	3,167	$406.8	3,082	$407.1	2,943	$435.5	2,774	$438.7	2,569	$457.1
924	143.2	950	147.3	910	144.4	884	152.3	812	153.5	763	159.1
1,810	250.1	2,217	259.5	2,172	262.7	2,059	283.3	1,962	285.3	1,806	298.0
1,817	254.7	1,920	274.1	1,943	292.1	1,837	291.5	1,801	297.7	1,772	315.1
1,122	178.0	1,159	188.8	1,218	210.8	1,171	210.5	1,176	217.8	1,185	230.8
695	76.7	761	85.2	725	81.3	666	81.0	625	79.9	587	84.4
894	138.6	947	145.3	792	122.4	768	123.1	730	138.5	763	146.3
657	111.1	701	117.4	559	96.3	553	96.6	533	111.4	557	117.8
237	27.6	246	27.9	233	26.1	215	26.5	197	27.1	206	28.6
570	85.6	596	87.7	592	83.5	571	90.5	538	89.6	537	94.7
323	55.7	341	57.1	346	54.5	330	55.4	321	54.8	318	58.4
247	29.9	255	30.5	246	28.9	241	35.1	217	34.8	219	36.4
1,407	180.0	1,432	193.4	1,376	191.1	1,367	215.0	1,328	220.6	1,358	230.7
965	131.5	968	140.4	935	140.6	970	163.3	929	165.2	952	172.3
442	48.5	464	52.9	441	50.5	397	51.7	399	55.4	406	58.4
221	39.3	226	40.4	207	39.7	187	40.2	190	40.7	183	42.1
0	180.9	0	158.3	0	175.3	0	169.3	0	182.1	0	204.8
668	82.0	652	84.1	575	90.2	508	87.2	532	85.7	523	91.8
8,311	$1,354.4	8,940	$1,390.1	8,567	$1,401.2	8,181	$1,452.3	7,893	$1,493.6	7,705	$1,582.7

0	$0	0	$0	0	$0	0	$0	0	$0	0	$0
0	0	0	0	0	0	0	0	0	0	0	0
0	0	0	0	0	0	0	0	0	0	0	0
700	109.6	776	129.8	1,006	167.5	1,081	190.7	1,146	211.2	1,143	228.4
658	104.1	742	125.1	972	162.7	1,049	185.6	1,110	205.3	1,103	223.5
42	5.6	34	4.7	34	4.8	32	5.1	36	5.9	40	5.0
242	39.2	282	48.1	246	44.7	273	47.6	249	59.2	282	55.8
237	38.3	274	47.1	238	43.6	265	46.4	239	57.5	270	54.3
5	1.0	8	1.0	8	1.1	8	1.1	10	1.7	12	1.6
0	0	0	0	3	1.0	39	8.0	54	8.0	51	11.0
0	0	0	0	3	1.0	39	8.0	54	8.0	51	11.0
0	0	0	0	0	0	0	0	0	0	0	0
47	13.7	53	23.9	139	30.4	149	29.3	170	34.5	186	36.9

Dollars in millions

	1998		1999		2000		2001	
	FTE	$	FTE	$	FTE	$	FTE	$
Center for Devices and Radiological Health	32	8.7	32	5.0	30	4.5	30	3.9
Office of Regulatory Affairs	19	5.2	16	8.3	16	8.1	15	8.4
National Center for Toxicological Research	0	0	0	0	0	0	0	0
Rent and F acilities^a	0	0	0	5.4	0	5.6	0	5.9
Other^c	115	12.7	203	18.9	174	17.3	173	17.8
Subtotal	825	$137.7	1,059	$144.7	1,102	$165.8	1,184	$178.8
Total	8,908	$1,069.6	8,910	$1,130.0	8,830	$1,214.0	8,989	$1,278.1

2002		2003		2004		2005		2006		2007	
FT E	$	FTE	$	F TE	$	FTE	$	FTE	$	FTE	$
32	4.9	35	14.7	126	21.3	134	19.9	156	24.6	172	26.5
15	8.8	18	9.2	13	9.1	15	9.5	14	9.9	14	10.4
0	0	0	0	0	0	0	0	0	0	0	0
0	1.0	0	9.2	0	11.3	0	25.9	0	30.1	0	30.0
168	19.0	206	26.5	180	22.9	187	24.2	186	25.9	202	29.3
1,157	$182.6	1,317	$237.6	1,574	$277.7	1,729	$325.2	1,805	$369.1	1,864	$391.4
9,468	$1,537.0	10,257	$1,627.7	10,141	$1,678.9	9,910	$1,777.5	9,698	$1,862.7	9,569	$1,974.1

Source: GAO analysis of FDA data.

^aIncludes GSA rent, other rent, rent-related activities, White Oak Consolidation, and the FDA Buildings and Facilities Appropriation. bIncludes tobacco program, Office of the Commissioner, Office of Policy, Office of External Affairs, Office of Operations/Orphan Grants Administration, Office of Management and Systems, and Central Services. cOther activities funded in part by user fees, including Office of the Commissioner, Office of Policy, Office of External Affairs, Office of Operations/Orphan Grants Administration, Office of Management and Systems, Central Services, Export Certification, and Color Certification Fund.

APPENDIX V: FDA'S ADMINISTRATION OF HEALTH CLAIMS IN RESPONSE TO THE PEARSON V. SHALALA RULING

The Nutrition Labeling and Education Act of 1990 (NLEA)1 amended the Federal Food, Drug, and Cosmetic Act [2] to include provisions that govern the use of health claims on food labeling. For conventional foods, the NLEA requires that any claim that expressly or by implication characterizes the relationship of a nutrient to a disease or health-related condition must be authorized by the

Secretary of Health and Human Services (delegated to FDA) through a regulation [3] Under the NLEA, FDA may authorize a health claim for a conventional food if it determines, based on the totality of publicly available scientific evidence, that there is "significant scientific agreement" among experts—qualified by scientific training and experience to evaluate such claims—that the claim is supported by such evidence. Although the NLEA also provided for the use of health claims in dietary supplement labeling, Congress did not require dietary supplement health claims to be subject to the same statutory procedures and standards as conventional food health claims. Instead, dietary supplement health claims were to be subject to procedures and standards established in regulations issued by the Secretary of Health and Human Services (delegated to FDA).

In 1991, FDA published a proposed rule in the Federal Register, proposing the implementation of the statutory procedures and standards for health claims for conventional food, and proposing to adopt those same procedures and standards for dietary supplement health claims [4]. However, before the rule could be finalized, Congress passed legislation that generally prohibited FDA from implementing the NLEA with respect to dietary supplements until December 15, 1993 [5]. Therefore, in January of 1993, when FDA adopted the final rules for health claims for conventional foods, it did not finalize rules for dietary supplement health claims [6]. However, 1 year later, after the prohibition of implementation of NLEA for dietary supplements had expired, FDA adopted a rule that subjected dietary supplement health claims to the same general requirements that applied to conventional foods [7]. Under those rules, any person wanting to include a health claim on a conventional food or dietary supplement label must petition FDA for authorization before including the claim on the label. If FDA determines, based on the totality of publicly available information, that there is significant scientific agreement in support of that claim, it will authorize its use by issuing it in regulation.

FDA's health claim regulations for dietary supplements were the subject of several lawsuits in the 1990s. In a case known as Pearson v. Shalala, [8] the U.S. Court of Appeals for the District of Columbia Circuit held that the First Amendment does not permit FDA to prohibit a potentially misleading health claim on the label of a dietary supplement, unless FDA considers whether a disclaimer on the product's label could negate the potentially misleading nature of that claim. Specifically, the court stated that although inherently or actually misleading information in food labeling or advertising may be prohibited, potentially misleading information cannot face an absolute prohibition. Instead, potentially misleading information may be regulated only if those regulations directly advance a substantial government interest, and offer a reasonable fit between the government's goals and the means chosen to accomplish those goals. The court found a substantial interest in protecting the public health and preventing consumer fraud. However, it found that FDA's regulation requiring health claims to be supported by significant scientific agreement did not directly advance the interest in public health, and, even though the regulations directly advanced the interest in preventing consumer fraud, the fit between the goals of the regulations and the means employed—an outright ban without the possibility of a disclaimer—was not reasonable [9].

Following the decision in Pearson, FDA announced its plan to respond, stating that it would deny, without prejudice, all petitions for the use of dietary supplement health claims that did not meet the significant scientific agreement standard while the agency conducted and completed a rulemaking to reconsider the procedures and standards governing such claims [10]. Then, according to FDA, once a rule was finalized, the agency would revisit the petitions it had denied. However, in 2000, citing concerns over additional First Amendment challenges, FDA announced plans to modify that policy [11]. FDA stated that it would continue to approve dietary supplement health claims that met the significant scientific agreement standard, but it would exercise its enforcement discretion and not take action against dietary supplement health claims that failed to meet the standard under certain circumstances. Specifically, upon the submission of a valid petition for preapproval of a dietary supplement health claim, if FDA did not find significant scientific agreement, but, in evaluating the weight of the evidence, did find that the scientific evidence in support of the claim outweighed the scientific evidence against it, and consumer health and safety were not threatened, the agency would inform the petitioner of conditions under which the agency would refrain from taking enforcement action against the health claim. If the scientific evidence against the health claim outweighed the scientific evidence in support of it, FDA would deny any use of the health claim.

Then, in 2002, the agency announced the availability of guidance, updating its approach to implementing the Pearson decision [12]. In large part, the procedures remained the same; however, FDA included health claims for conventional foods under the procedures, even though the Pearson case directly addressed only dietary supplements. FDA stated that it believed that such a move would precipitate greater communication in food labeling and thereby enhance public health. In addition, FDA stated that including health claims for conventional foods in its enforcement discretion policy would help avoid further constitutional challenges. Subsequently, in 2003, FDA announced the availability of two new guidance documents describing interim procedures that, among other things, addressed a then recent U.S. District Court for the District of Columbia decision that found the weight of the evidence standard that FDA first articulated in guidance in 2000 was inappropriate [13]. According to the district court in that case, FDA should evaluate qualified health claims based on the presence of "credible evidence," not the weight of the evidence [14]. The 2003 guidance documents set forth new procedures for qualified health claims for conventional foods and dietary supplements. Specifically, qualified health claim petitions would be evaluated using an evidence-based ranking system that would rate the strength of the publicly available scientific evidence. A claim would be denied if there was no credible evidence to support it. Otherwise, based on the competent and reliable scientific evidence in support, a claim would be assigned to one of four ranked levels—the first level being "significant scientific agreement among qualified experts" and the remaining three levels being for claims supported by some lower level of credible evidence. Each of the three categories not ranked as supported by significant scientific agreement would correspond to one of three standardized qualifying statements (i.e., disclaimers) [15]. So long as the qualified health claim bore the appropriate language, met other applicable health claim regulations, and adhered to criteria established in FDA's letter of enforcement discretion in response to the petition, FDA would exercise its enforcement discretion and refrain from acting against the health claim.

In November of 2003, FDA published an Advance Notice of Proposed Rulemaking, recognizing the need to establish transparent, long-term procedures that have the effect of law [16]. In that announcement, FDA presented several regulatory alternatives: (1) incorporate the interim procedures and evidence-based ranking system we have previously discussed into regulation; (2) subject health claims to notice-and-comment rulemaking, as before Pearson, but reinterpret the "significant scientific agreement" standard to refer to the evidence supporting the claim being made, instead of the underlying substance-disease relationship; or (3) treat qualified health claims as outside the NLEA and regulate them on a postmarket basis (i.e., pursue the product as misbranded if the health claim renders the label false or misleading because the claim lacks substantiation). FDA does not plan to work on this proposed rulemaking this year. In May of 2006, FDA issued guidance concerning FDA's implementation of qualified health claims process. In that guidance, FDA reaffirmed the 2003 interim procedures and stated that "FDA is currently considering various options regarding the development of proposed regulations related to qualified health claims," and "...[i]n the meantime, the agency plans to review qualified health claim petitions on a case-bycase basis." [17].

APPENDIX VI:
COMMENTS FROM THE FOOD AND DRUG ADMINISTRATION

Note: GAO comments supplementing those in the report text appear at the end of this appendix.

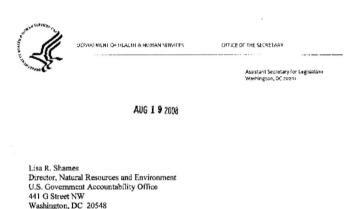

DEPARTMENT OF HEALTH & HUMAN SERVICES   OFFICE OF THE SECRETARY

Assistant Secretary for Legislation
Washington, DC 20201

AUG 1 9 2008

Lisa R. Shames
Director, Natural Resources and Environment
U.S. Government Accountability Office
441 G Street NW
Washington, DC 20548

Dear Ms. Shames:

Enclosed are the Department's comments on U.S. Government Accountability Office's (GAO) draft report entitled: "Food Labeling: FDA Needs to Better Leverage Resources, Improve Oversight, and Effectively Use Available Data to Help Consumers Select Healthy Foods" (GAO 08-597).

The Department appreciates the opportunity to review and comment on this report before its publication.

Sincerely,

Vincent J. Ventimiglia, Jr.
Assistant Secretary for Legislation

Attachment

GENERAL COMMENTS FOR THE DEPARTMENT OF HEALTH AND HUMAN SERVICES (HHS) ON THE U.S. GOVERNMENT ACCOUNTABILITY OFFICE'S (GAO) DRAFT REPORT ENTITLED: "FOOD LABELING — FDA NEEDS TO BETTER LEVERAGE RESOURCES, IMPROVE OVERSIGHT, AND EFFECTIVELY USE AVAILABLE DATA TO HELP CONSUMERS SELECT HEALTHY FOODS" (GAO-08-597)

The Food and Drug Administration (FDA) appreciates the opportunity to review and comment on the Government Accountability Office's (GAO) draft report. While GAO has raised some important issues regarding the regulation of food labeling, FDA does not believe that the report places food labeling in the appropriate context given the agency's overall public health mission, and the multitude of competing priorities it faces. Specifically, the FDA endeavors to "better leverage resources, improve oversight, and effectively use available data to help consumers select healthy foods." Further, GAO's findings fail to account for all the varied initiatives that FDA and the Department of Health and Human Services (HHS) have undertaken to fight obesity and ensure that foods are labeled in a manner that fosters consumer education and healthy choices.

Food Safety and the Food Protection Plan

Throughout the GAO report, reference is made to food labeling being a part of FDA's food safety mission. Food labeling informs the consumer about the basic nature, characteristics, and other attributes, such as nutritional content, of a food. Although there may be some aspects of food labeling that can affect the safe use of the food, e.g., alerting allergic consumers to ingredients they need to avoid or providing information on how to safely handle, cook, or store a food, food labeling does not describe the food's safety, nor can it be used to determine the safety of a food product. In light of the different issues involved, including different statutory authority, FDA generally treats and staffs food safety and food labeling as separate areas of responsibility.

The report refers to the Food Protection Plan (FPP) several times. The references imply that the provisions of the FPP are specifically focused on and/or directed to deal with issues related to false or misleading labeling. The FPP was designed to address food safety and defense concerns. Some of the actions *may* have *some* bearing on food labeling issues, but food labeling concerns were not the focus or impetus for developing the plan or for the plan's requested new authorities for FDA. The multiple references to the FPP throughout the report present a false impression that the FPP is either principally or substantially about food labeling.

Resources, Priorities, and Information Technology

The report states that GAO did not assess how efficiently FDA used its resources or the impact of competing priorities when evaluating FDA's approach to the problem of misleading food labeling. However, these issues are central to all FDA regulatory decisions, including those regarding food labeling. With the exception of food labeling violations that concern the presence of major food allergens, most misleading food labeling violations do not present a high risk to public health. Nevertheless, our field force frequently conducts labeling examinations during their inspection and investigative activities. For example, continuous efforts are made to ensure that required labeling is in English, and that it conforms to other specifications that help consumers in their purchasing decisions.

GENERAL COMMENTS FOR THE DEPARMENT OF HEALTH AND HUMAN SERVICES (HHS) ON THE U.S. GOVERNMENT ACCOUNTABILITY OFFICE'S (GAO) DRAFT REPORT ENTITLED: "FOOD LABELING — FDA NEEDS TO BETTER LEVERAGE RESOURCES, IMPROVE OVERSIGHT, AND EFFECTIVELY USE AVAILABLE DATA TO HELP CONSUMERS SELECT HEALTHY FOODS" (GAO-08-597)

Another tool we rely upon is targeted sampling. FDA believes that targeted sample collection is the best use of agency resources for identifying misleading food labeling violations. Risk-based targeted sampling is the most valuable approach in all regulatory areas, including such examples as testing leafy greens and seafood for bacteria that cause foodborne illness. Random sampling is not, however, an efficient use of agency resources, except in limited circumstances where the agency believes it is important to establish baseline data.

Regarding GAO's concerns about FDA's information technology (IT) systems, we have several initiatives underway to improve those systems, and to ensure that they support our business processes. IT systems support our research, risk assessments, inspection, surveillance and other activities, and are designed to serve those needs. FDA has developed strategic plans to respond to high-profile challenges in priority areas. FDA is committed to our mission and committed to effecting beneficial changes necessary to protect America's public health. FDA does not believe that tracking and analyzing data and providing routine reports on food labeling violations is the best use of agency resources, given the vast array of competing priorities confronting the agency.

Finally, when FDA learned of the discrepancy between the warning letters issued and the warning letters posted on the website, FDA engaged in an intense and thorough reconciliation process, and continues to proactively work to put measures into place to prevent such discrepancies from occurring in the future. The Division of Freedom and Information (DFOI) and the Office of Regulatory Affairs (ORA) continue to conduct audits of the agency's warning letter database.

FDA Comments on GAO Recommendations

Recommendation: Ensure that labeling office managers have the information they need to oversee compliance with food labeling statutes and regulations by

- *Maintaining, in a searchable format, data on food labeling violations, including type of violation, information about corrective actions taken or, if no action was taken, the reason why;*
- *Analyzing violation data in routine management reports; and*
- *Tracking untitled letters and regulatory meetings related to food labeling violations and analyze whether these are an effective use of resources.*

FDA Response: FDA agrees that being able to track any and all information that would allow its investigators to better do their jobs would be useful to the agency. However, it is important to remember that data collection requires time and effort. It is important to make sure that data-entry does not become so burdensome that it takes away from other investigative work.

Recommendation: Ensure that the public has timely access to information on food labeling violations that may have serious health consequences by requiring all the centers and offices to post on FDA's public website, within a specified time frame, key information such as

2

GENERAL COMMENTS FOR THE DEPARMENT OF HEALTH AND HUMAN SERVICES (HHS) ON THE U.S. GOVERNMENT ACCOUNTABILITY OFFICE'S (GAO) DRAFT REPORT ENTITLED: "FOOD LABELING — FDA NEEDS TO BETTER LEVERAGE RESOURCES, IMPROVE OVERSIGHT, AND EFFECTIVELY USE AVAILABLE DATA TO HELP CONSUMERS SELECT HEALTHY FOODS" (GAO-08-597)

- *All warning letters;*
- *All recalls;*
- *Statistics on serious enforcement actions (e.g. import refusals) by country, type of food, and the problem found (e.g. undeclared allergen); and*
- *Information on violations that FDA classifies as serious (e.g. product identification, exposure symptoms)*

FDA Response: FDA already posts and maintains much of this information on its website. FDA will keep the information as up to date as possible given resource and time limitations.

FDA's Detention Authority for Foods

In several places throughout the draft GAO report, it is suggested that the only context in which FDA detains food is under the Public Health Security and Bioterrorism Preparedness and Response Act of 2002 (Bioterrorism Act). While the Bioterrorism Act gives FDA authority to administratively detain an article of food if certain conditions are met, the report should clearly note that FDA has another type of detention authority under section 801 of the Federal Food, Drug, and Cosmetic Act (FFDCA). This second type of detention authority applies to imported articles, including food, which appears to violate the FFDCA. The two types of authority are outlined below.

FFDCA 801(a) — When FDA initiates refusal of admission under section 801(a) because it has made an initial determination that a food offered for import appears to violate the FFDCA, the food is said to be "detained" pending a final decision as to its admissibility. While the food is under detention, the importer has an opportunity to introduce testimony and, in some circumstances, can request authorization to bring the product into compliance. After this process, the product will ultimately be admitted into domestic commerce or refused admission. In this context, detention thus refers to withholding release of a product pending a decision regarding admission or refusal.

FFDCA 304(h) — Section 304(h) covers any article of food that presents a threat of serious adverse health consequences or death to humans or animals. Although section 304(h) was added to the FFDCA by the Bioterrorism Act, an act or threat of terrorism is not required to use the authority. Credible evidence or information indicating that the article presents a threat of serious health consequences or death is the evidentiary standard for using this authority. See 21 CFR Part 1, subpart K, and FFDCA section 304(h). FDA has not yet used its detention authority under the Bioterrorism Act because, to date, FDA has been able to use other authorities and regulatory tools to adequately protect the public health. Although the section 304(h) authority applies to both domestic and imported food, FDA expects to use this authority principally for domestic food. If imported food is subject to administrative detention under section 304(h), it is very likely also subject to detention and refusal of admission under section 801(a), as described above.

3

<u>**GENERAL COMMENTS FOR THE DEPARMENT OF HEALTH AND HUMAN SERVICES (HHS) ON THE U.S. GOVERNMENT ACCOUNTABILITY OFFICE'S (GAO) DRAFT REPORT ENTITLED: "FOOD LABELING — FDA NEEDS TO BETTER LEVERAGE RESOURCES, IMPROVE OVERSIGHT, AND EFFECTIVELY USE AVAILABLE DATA TO HELP CONSUMERS SELECT HEALTHY FOODS" (GAO-08-597)**</u>

Nutrition Labeling, Nutrition Symbols, and Consumer Research

Concerning the report's recommendation that FDA develop a simplified system for conveying the overall nutritional quality of a food to consumers, here is some background on how FDA's current nutrition labeling requirements came into existence and on the agency's consumer research in this area. In 1990 Congress amended the FFDCA by enacting the Nutrition Labeling and Education Act of 1990 (NLEA) (Public Law 101-535, 104 Stat. 2353). NLEA established mandatory nutrition labeling for packaged foods to enable consumers to make more informed and healthier food product choices in the context of their daily diets. The United States was likely the first government to institute mandatory nutrition labeling for packaged foods. In 1993, FDA issued regulations implementing the NLEA. Prior to issuing these regulations, FDA conducted consumer research to determine how best to meet the objectives of the new law. Based on this research, FDA established a standardized format in a tabular form for the nutrition label so that consumers could readily recognize and become familiar with the nutrition information provided in labeling. It included nutrients to limit in the diet (e.g. saturated fat, sodium), as well as nutrients that consumers need in their diet (e.g. vitamin A, fiber). This section of the label is referred to as Nutrition Facts and is well recognized by consumers. The research also resulted in the decision to include a benchmark, the percent Daily Value (%DV), for consumers in the Nutrition Facts so that they could readily compare products and could judge how a product fits into their overall diet. The %DV has facilitated the development of education programs on the use of the Nutrition Facts for planning healthful diets and is integrated into the *Dietary Guidelines for Americans*.

Among the regulations to implement NLEA, the agency set forth general principles for nutrient content claims (21 CFR 101.13), which are claims that characterize the level of a nutrient in a food (e.g., "low fat," "good source of fiber"), and for health claims (21 CFR 101.14), which are claims that characterize the relationship of a food substance to a disease or health-related condition (e.g., "calcium may reduce the risk of osteoporosis"). Once such claims have been authorized by FDA, manufacturers may use them in food labeling, when products are eligible. The agency has been aware that in recent years there has been a trend in food labeling to use symbols and icons on the label to indicate the nutritional attributes and quality of the food product; however, the agency lacked adequate information about how various symbols are understood and used by consumers, and how symbols may affect food choices available in the marketplace.

FDA received a petition from a consumer organization requesting that the agency explore the use of front-of-package symbols to convey the healthfulness of foods (Docket No. 2006P-0498). After receiving the petition, the agency held a public hearing to afford industry, consumers, and other interested parties the opportunity to provide research and comments on the use of symbols to communicate nutrition information on food labels. The public hearing notice outlined three main issues and posed questions for each of these issues. The first issue was concerned with the types of foods that bear nutrition symbols and the nutrient requirements for those symbols. The second issue was concerned with consumer understanding and use of nutrition symbols. The third issue was concerned with the economic impacts of nutrition symbols on food labels. The agency is currently evaluating the information received and the necessary next steps.

4

GENERAL COMMENTS FOR THE DEPARMENT OF HEALTH AND HUMAN SERVICES (HHS) ON THE U.S. GOVERNMENT ACCOUNTABILITY OFFICE'S (GAO) DRAFT REPORT ENTITLED: "FOOD LABELING — FDA NEEDS TO BETTER LEVERAGE RESOURCES, IMPROVE OVERSIGHT, AND EFFECTIVELY USE AVAILABLE DATA TO HELP CONSUMERS SELECT HEALTHY FOODS" (GAO-08-597)

CFSAN is also taking steps to better understand how consumers interpret and use front-of-package nutrition symbols and how these symbols affect food choices. Its Office of Regulations, Policy, and Social Sciences (ORPSS) received funding to conduct two studies for FY07 and FY08. The first FY07 study (Consumer Perceptions of Nutrition Quality Indicators) is complete, and included four focus groups (two in Calverton, MD and two in Albany, NY) with adult respondents. The purpose of these groups was to evaluate consumers' reactions to a variety of front-of-package symbol schemes that are currently found in the marketplace, and to other front-of-package symbols that can potentially be used to communicate the nutritional characteristics of packaged foods. The findings from these groups will inform the experimental variables (i.e. conditions) selected for an upcoming Internet panel experiment (Evaluation of Nutrition Symbols on Food Packages) that will provide empirical information about accurate and erroneous judgments and inferences that consumers make in response to front-of-package symbols. The experiment will be designed to provide CFSAN's Office of Nutrition, Labeling and Dietary Supplements (ONLDS) with information about potential problems stemming from halo effects, information search truncation, and interactions between front-of-package symbols and other information on the food label, such as the Nutrition Facts panel (NFP), nutrient content claims, and health claims. Following the initial experimental study, we will use FY08 funds to conduct another round of focus groups (Qualitative Research on Consumer Response to Nutrition Symbols). The purpose of these groups will be to provide additional qualitative information about the front-of-package symbol schemes that were found to be most effective in the Internet panel experiment, and to discuss ways in which any problems related to misleading labeling might be addressed and remedied. The findings from these focus groups will be used to inform the conditions for the second Internet panel experiment (Consumer Responses to Nutrition Symbols), which will further evaluate the front-of-package symbol schemes from the first experiment that were found to most effectively communicate information to consumers about the nutritional characteristics of packaged foods. The second study will also evaluate possible remedies (e.g. disclosures, disclaimers) for any misleading effects that result from the use of front-of-package symbols.

CFSAN has findings from its nationally representative telephone surveys that provide important information on consumers' use of the Nutrition Facts Panel (NFP). Data from the 1996 and 2002 Health and Diet Surveys indicate that approximately 70% of adults say they look at the NFP the first time they purchase a food, and that the majority of these adults use the NFP to compare the nutrition profiles of similar types of products (e.g. cereals, frozen entrees) and to find the declared amounts for specific nutrients of concern (e.g. sodium, fats). Furthermore, findings from the NFP format studies conducted by CFSAN in the mid-1990's showed that even if consumers cannot define or do not completely understand a metric found on the NFP (e.g. Percent Daily Value, or %DV), they can still use that information to compare the nutrition profiles of two products and accurately determine which product is more healthful.

We agree with GAO's recommendation for empirical research to evaluate the communication effects of nutrition symbols, but believe it is important to extend our investigation beyond issues related to the consistency, accuracy, and effectiveness of the symbols. Specifically, CFSAN believes it is important to determine how consumers will use the symbols in combination with front-of-package claims and the NFP. We plan to examine how these different types of label information interact and influence consumers' decision-making. We also intend to determine whether the symbols lead to a truncation of consumers' information search, and whether these symbols result in "halo effects" that create misperceptions about unrelated product characteristics.

<u>GENERAL COMMENTS FOR THE DEPARMENT OF HEALTH AND HUMAN SERVICES</u>
<u>(HHS) ON THE U.S. GOVERNMENT ACCOUNTABILITY OFFICE'S (GAO) DRAFT REPORT</u>
<u>ENTITLED: "FOOD LABELING — FDA NEEDS TO BETTER LEVERAGE RESOURCES,</u>
<u>IMPROVE OVERSIGHT, AND EFFECTIVELY USE AVAILABLE DATA TO HELP</u>
<u>CONSUMERS SELECT HEALTHY FOODS" (GAO-08-597)</u>

Qualified Health Claims

The report notes, "Stakeholders, such as the American Heart Association (AHA), have suggested that FDA eliminate the use of qualified health claims on food labels" and states that findings from 2005 and 2007 FDA studies support the view that these claims may encourage consumption of foods with little or no health benefits. There are two problems with this discussion of qualified health claims. First, for completeness, the GAO report should note that court decisions, beginning with *Pearson v. Shalala*, hold that the First Amendment precludes FDA from prohibiting the use of a qualified health claim unless FDA can show that the claim is inherently misleading or, if the claim is only potentially misleading, that use of disclaimer would not remedy the claim's potential to mislead. Thus, absent consumer research or other evidence that satisfies the *Pearson* court's criteria, FDA does not have the authority to eliminate use of qualified health claims as a class of claims. Secondly, contrary to the statement in the report, FDA's 2005 and 2007 qualified health claim experiments did not find that qualified health claims might encourage the consumption of foods with little or no health benefits. This conclusion goes well beyond the data. FDA's research simply showed that qualified health claims produced halo effects, that consumers could not use "word only" qualifiers to determine the level of scientific support for different claims, and that while consumers could use report card grades to help them discriminate the level of scientific support between claims, these grades (i.e. qualifiers) did not remedy the halo effects resulting from the claims.

6

The following are GAO's comments on the Department of Health and Human Service's (HHS) letter dated August 19, 2008.

GAO COMMENTS

1. FDA commented that the report did not place food labeling in the appropriate context, given FDA's overall public health mission and competing priorities. We believe the food labeling responsibilities are part of that mission. The Federal Food, Drug, and Cosmetic Act specifically describes FDA's mission to include protecting the public health by, among other things, ensuring that "foods are safe, wholesome, sanitary, and properly labeled." FDA also commented that the report failed to account for all the varied initiatives that FDA and HHS have undertaken to fight obesity and ensure that foods are labeled in a manner that fosters consumer education and healthy choices. The subject of this report is food labeling, not obesity. With respect to labeling initiatives to help consumers make healthy food choices, the report identifies several areas where stakeholders believe that FDA falls short.

2. Although FDA said that it does not consider food labeling part of its food safety mission, it does include reviewing labels as a required step in a food safety inspection. Also, overseeing industry compliance with labeling requirements is part of FDA's food oversight responsibilities and labeling laws help consumers ensure that the food they buy is safe for them eat. That said, since FDA made this distinction, we revised the wording in some places in the final report.

3. FDA took issue with the report's frequent references to the Food Protection Plan. FDA stated that the plan was developed to address food safety and defense, although it may have some bearing on food labeling issues. It was not our intent to suggest that the plan's primary focus was on food labeling, and we have clarified this in the report. The report discusses the Plan's potential to help FDA carry out its food regulatory responsibilities and discusses certain provisions that, if implemented, may be useful tools in monitoring and enforcing the food labeling requirements.

4. FDA correctly noted that the report does not evaluate how efficiently FDA used its resources or the impact of its changing priorities, although we did examine resources for food labeling. For example, the report provides 10 years of budget data on FDA, with detailed data for each center, including (1) total staffing and funding, (2) the portion of Office of Regulatory Affairs' staffing and funding for inspections and other oversight, and (3) staffing and funding supported by user fees. However, because FDA was not able to provide risk-based priority plans or annual

work projections for all labeling activities, we could not determine how efficiently labeling resources were used or the impact of changing priorities on labeling.

5. FDA contended that most misleading food labeling violations do not present a high risk to public health. However, FDA has not conducted the research to identify which food labels are misleading and therefore has little or no basis for determining the health impacts of misleading labeling violations.

6. FDA commented that it does not believe that tracking and analyzing data and providing routine reports on food labeling violations is the best use of its resources, given competing priorities. We maintain that risk-based decisions, such as allocating resources effectively, must include careful analysis of this type of data on regulatory programs. Moreover, FDA already collects most of these data so resource investment to generate the reports should be minimal and worth the benefits of ensuring that managers' decisions are well-informed and risk-based. As FDA rolls out several initiatives for improving its information technology systems, which it states are under way, HHS may want to provide FDA managers with training on using the systems as management tools.

7. FDA said it agreed that being able to track any and all information that would allow its investigators to better do their jobs would be useful to the agency, but that data collection requires time and effort. FDA continued, it is important to make sure that data entry does not become so burdensome that it takes away from other investigative work. However, as we previously noted, FDA already collects most of these data. With a small resource investment, analyzing these data in reports can help managers make more informed decisions.

8. FDA implied that it may not have the resources to keep data on the public Web site up to date. However, providing consumers with information that is timely and complete can help them avoid potentially dangerous food and make healthy food purchases.

9. FDA commented that the report suggests in several places that the only context in which FDA detains food is under the Bioterrorism Act, and that that FDA has another type of detention authority that applies to imported articles. However, the report does discuss FDA's other detention authority under section 801(a) of the Federal Food, Drug, and Cosmetic Act. The report refers to these actions as "import refusals," which is the term that FDA currently uses for these enforcement actions. We added a footnote in the text to note this.

10. FDA's statement—that its survey indicated that 70 percent of adults said they look at the Nutrition Facts panel the first time they purchase a food—is misleading. In that survey, 44 percent of respondents told FDA that they "often" read the panel the first time they purchase a food, and 25 percent "sometimes" read the panel at that time; while 31 percent "rarely" or "never" read the panel.

11. FDA commented that (1) court decisions, beginning with Pearson v. Shalala, hold that the First Amendment precludes FDA from prohibiting the use of qualified health claims unless FDA can show that the claim is inherently misleading, or if the claim is only potentially misleading, that the use of a disclaimer would not remedy the claim's potential to mislead, and (2) that absent consumer research or other evidence that satisfies the criteria set by the court in Pearson v. Shalala, FDA does not have the authority to eliminate qualified health claims as a class of claims. We added language to the report to acknowledge FDA's position.

FDA commented that, contrary to our report, FDA's 2005 and 2007 qualified health claims experiments did not find that qualified health claims might encourage the consumption of foods with little or no health benefits. Our report states that, according to the stakeholders we consulted, "... these claims confuse or mislead consumers and may encourage consumption of foods with little or no health benefits." It then states that "[t]his view was supported by findings from 2005 and 2007 FDA studies." This statement is consistent with FDA's findings. According to its public Web site, those studies on qualified health claims found that "qualifying statements ... were not understood by consumers" and "even when ... understood as intended, qualifying statements had unexpected effects on consumers' judgments about the health benefits and overall healthfulness .... "

REFERENCES

[1]   Go to http://www.MyPyramid.gov to view USDA's 2005 revised food guide pyramid— entitled *MyPyramid*—and access hyperlinks to other nutrition information sponsored by the federal government.

[2]   21 U.S.C. §§ 301-399.

[3]   GAO, *High-Risk Series: An Update,* GAO-07-310 (Washington, D.C.: January 2007).

[4]   HHS, FDA, *FDA Science and Mission at Risk* (Washington, D.C.: November 2007).

[5] HHS, FDA, *Food Protection Plan: An Integrated Strategy for Protecting the Nation's Food Supply* (Washington, D.C.: November 2007).

[6] FDA's Commissioner provided the assessment of immediate resource needs in a May 3, 2008, letter in response to a request from the Ranking Member, Subcommittee on Labor, Health and Human Services, Education, and Related Agencies, Senate Committee on Appropriations.

[7] GAO, *Federal Oversight of Food Safety: FDA Has Provided Few Details on the Resources and Strategies Needed to Implement its Food Protection Plan*, GAO-08-909T (Washington, D.C.: June 12, 2008); and *Federal Oversight of Food Safety: FDA's Food Protection Plan Proposes Positive First Steps, but Capacity to Carry Them Out Is Critical*, GAO-08-435T (Washington, D.C.: Jan. 29, 2008).

[8] GAO, *Federal User Fees: A Design Guide*, GAO-08-386SP (Washington, D.C.: May 29, 2008).

[9] GAO, *Food Safety: USDA and FDA Need to Better Ensure Prompt and Complete Recalls of Potentially Unsafe Food*, GAO-05-51 (Washington, D.C.: Oct. 6, 2004)

[10] GAO-08-386SP.

[11] Certain small businesses are exempt from certain labeling requirements and other exceptions exist—for example, packaged fresh fruits or vegetables, in which nutrients vary depending on growing conditions, are not generally required to include a Nutrition Facts panel.

[12] Dietary supplements have different labeling requirements.

[13] On labels for products distributed solely in Puerto Rico or in a U.S. Territory where the predominant language is not English, the predominant language may be substituted for English.

[14] GAO-05-51.

[15] A food product entry line is each portion of a shipment that is a separate type of product.

[16] Life Sciences Research Office, Federation of American Societies for Experimental Biology. "Analytical Data and Label Review of 300 Food Products" (Bethesda, MD: October 1994).

[17] To access warning letter data on FDA's public Web site, go to http://www.fda.gov/foi/warning.htm.

[18] GAO, *Mad Cow Disease: FDA's Management of the Feed Ban Has Improved, but Oversight Weaknesses Continue to Limit Program Effectiveness*, GAO-05-101 (Washington, D.C.: Feb. 25, 2005).

[19] After fiscal year 2007 ended, FDA obtained another consent decree of permanent injunction prohibiting Brownwood Acres Foods, Inc., from

promoting its fruit products and dietary supplements with unauthorized health claims and unapproved drug claims.

[20] FDA currently uses the term "import refusals" for its detention authority under section 801(a) of the Federal Food, Drug, and Cosmetic Act.

[21] According to FDA officials, there may also be shipments that were detained for labeling violations, reconditioned by the owner, and then released.

[22] GAO-05-51

[23] GAO-08-909T

[24] The department's 2009 justification also proposed user fees for issuing food and animal feed export certificates—a proposal recommended in the Food Protection Plan.

[25] GAO-08-386SP

[26] GAO, *Medical Devices: FDA Faces Challenges in Conducting Inspections of Foreign Manufacturing Establishments*, GAO-08-780T (Washington, D.C.: May 14, 2008).

[27] GAO-05-51.

[28] GAO-08-435T and GAO-08-909T.

[29] Gill Cowburn and Lynn Stockley, *Consumer Understanding and Use of Nutrition Labeling: a Systematic Review*, Public Health Nutrition (University of Oxford: August 2004). This comprehensive synthesis reported on 103 studies. Using a set protocol and standard published criteria, the authors judged 9 percent of the studies to be of high or medium-high quality. This study also included studies from other countries that have less nutrition labeling than the United States. We determined this synthesis was sufficiently reliable for our purposes.

[30] National Academies, Institute of Medicine, *Food Marketing to Children and Youth: Threat or Opportunity?*, National Academies Press (Washington, D.C.: 2006).

[31] For information on this proposal, go to the following Web site: http://www.europarl.europa.eu/oeil/FindByDocnum.do?lang=en&docnum=COM/2008/40.

[32] FDA, *Experimental Study of Qualified Health Claims: Consumer Inferences about Monounsaturated Fatty Acids from Olive Oil, EPA and DHA Omega-3 Fatty Acids, and Green Tea (2007)*. FDA, Brenda Derby and Alan Levy, *Effects of Strength of Science Disclaimers on the Communication Impacts of Health Claims* (September 2005).

[33] FDA, "*Draft Guidance for Industry and FDA Staff: Whole Grain Label Statements*" (Feb. 17, 2006).

[34] National Academies, Institute of Medicine, *Preventing Childhood Obesity: Health in the Balance*, National Academies Press (Washington, D.C.: 2005)

[35] GAO-08-386SP.

Appendix I

[1] A "medical food" is a food that is formulated to be consumed or administered internally under the supervision of a physician, and that is intended for the specific dietary management of a disease or condition for which distinctive nutritional requirements, based on recognized scientific principles, are established by medical evaluation. An example of a medical food is an infant formula that is free of certain amino acids and is designed for infants with a rare genetic condition.

Appendix V

[2] Pub. L. No. 101-535, 104 Stat. 2353.

[3] 21 U.S.C. §§ 301-397.

[4] In addition, a claim may be authorized if a relevant scientific body of the U.S. government or the National Academies, or a subdivision thereof, has published an authoritative statement, currently in effect, about the relationship between a nutrient and a disease or health-related condition to which the claim refers.

[5] 56 Fed. Reg. 60,537, Nov. 27, 1991.

[6] Dietary Supplement Act of 1992, Pub. L. No. 102-571, tit. II § 202, 106 Stat. 4500. 58 Fed. Reg. 2478, Jan. 6, 1993.

[7] 59 Fed. Reg. 395, Jan. 4, 1994.

[8] 164 F.3d 650 (1999).

[9] In addition, the court found that the Administrative Procedure Act requires that FDA give some "definitional content to the phrase 'significant scientific agreement,'" either in regulation or on a case-by-case basis so that the regulated class can "perceive the principles which are guiding agency action." 164 F.3d at 661. FDA subsequently provided guidance describing the meaning of the phrase

[10] 64 Fed. Reg. 67,289, Dec. 1, 1999.

[11] 65 Fed. Reg. 59,855, Oct. 6, 2000.

[12] 67 Fed. Reg. 78,002, Dec. 20, 2002.

[13] 68 Fed. Reg. 41,387, July 11, 2003.

[14] *Whitaker v. Thompson*, 248 F. Supp. 2d 1 (2002). See also *Pearson v. Shalala*, 130 F. Supp. 2d 105 (2001).

[15] Those qualifying statements being (1) "although there is scientific evidence supporting the claim, the evidence is not conclusive"; (2) "some scientific evidence suggests ... however, FDA has determined that this evidence is limited and not conclusive"; and (3) "very little and preliminary scientific research suggests ... FDA concludes that there is little scientific evidence supporting this claim." FDA, *Interim Procedures for Qualified Health Claims in the Labeling of Conventional Human Foods and Human Dietary Supplements* (July 10, 2003).

[16] 68 Fed. Reg. 66,040, Nov. 25, 2003.

[17] FDA, Center for Food Safety and Applied Nutrition, *FDA's Implementation of "Qualified Health Claims": Questions and Answers* (May 12, 2006).

In: Food Labelling: FDA's Role...
Editor: Ethan C. Lefevre, pp. 71-79

ISBN 978-1-60692-898-1
© 2009 Nova Science Publishers, Inc.

Chapter 2

FOOD AND DRUG ADMINISTRATION (FDA): OVERVIEW AND ISSUES[*]

Erin D. Williams

ABSTRACT

The Food and Drug Administration (FDA) is the agency within the Department of Health and Human Services (HHS) that regulates human and animal drugs, medical devices, biologics, and most foods. This report describes FDA, surveys agency-related issues Congress faces, and cites CRS reports where readers can find more information.

FDA OVERVIEW

FDA is an agency within HHS that regulates a wide range of products valued at more than $1 trillion. (See Table 1.) The agency is responsible for the safety of most foods (human and animal) and cosmetics, and it regulates both the safety and the effectiveness of human drugs, biologics (e.g., vaccines, blood and blood components), medical devices, and animal drugs.

---

[*] Excerpted from CRS Report RS22946, dated September 8, 2008.

Table 1. What FDA Does and Does Not Regulate

Product or Activity	Regulatory Agency
Advertising	Federal Trade Commission (FTC) (FDA regulates prescription drug and restricted device advertising)
Alcohol	Treasury Department's Bureau of Alcohol, Tobacco, Firearms and Explosives
Biologics	FDA
Consumer products (e.g., toys, cigarette lighters, power tools)	Consumer Product Safety Commission
Cosmetics	FDA
Drinking water	EPA (FDA regulates bottled water)
Drugs	FDA (Drug Enforcement Administration regulates illegal drug use)
Foods	FDA (U.S. Department of Agriculture's (USDA's) Food Safety and Inspection Service regulates most meat and poultry and some egg products)
Health insurance	Centers for Medicare and Medicaid Services and state authorities
Medical Devices	FDA
Organ transplantation	HHS's Organ Procurement Transplantation Network
Pesticides	Environmental Protection Agency (EPA) (FDA and USDA regulate pesticides in food according to EPA's allowable levels)
Radiation-emitting electronic products	FDA
Restaurants and grocery stores	State and local food safety officials
Animal foods, feeds, drugs and devices	FDA (USDA regulates animal biologics)

Source: Adapted from "What FDA Regulates," at [http://www.fda.gov/comments/ regs.html], and "What FDA Does Not Regulate," at [http://www.fda.gov/comments /noregs.html].

In many cases, its responsibilities abut those of other agencies. (See Table 1.) In such cases, interagency agreements may define the regulatory boundaries.

The primary law authorizing FDA activities is the Federal Food, Drug, and Cosmetic Act (FFDCA; 21 USC Chapter 9). (See Table 2.) FDA is also responsible for implementing provisions in other laws, most notably the Public Health Service Act (PHSA; 42 USC Chapter 6A). For example, FDA's authority to regulate most human biologics flows both from the PHSA (§351) and from the FFDCA. (See Table 2)

Table 2. Location of Subjects Within the FFDCA

FFDCA	Subject
Chapter I	Short Title
Chapter II	Definitions
Chapter III	Prohibited Acts and Penalties
Chapter IV	Food
Chapter V Subchapter A Subchapter B Subchapter C Subchapter D Subchapter E Subchapter F	Drugs and Devices Drugs and Devices Drugs for Rare Diseases and Conditions Electronic Product Radiation Control Dissemination of Treatment Information General Provisions Relating to Drugs and Devices New Animal Drugs for Minor Use and Minor Species
Chapter VI	Cosmetics
Chapter VII Subchapter A Subchapter B Subchapter C Subchapter D Subchapter E Subchapter F Subchapter G Subchapter H Subchapter I	General Authority General Administrative Provisions Colors Fees Information and Education Environmental Impact Review National Uniformity for Nonprescription Drugs and Preemption for Labeling or Packaging of Cosmetics Safety Reports Serious Adverse Event Reports Reagan-Udall Foundation for the Food and Drug Administration
Chapter VIII	Imports and Exports
Chapter IX	Miscellaneous

FDA has three offices that perform agency-wide functions. The Office of the Commissioner conducts overall agency coordination. The Commissioner, FDA's top official, requires Senate confirmation. The Office of Chief Counsel handles the agency's legal needs. FDA's largest office, the Office of Regulatory Affairs (ORA), handles FDA's inspection and enforcement activities. It employs about one-third of the agency's personnel.

FDA's product-specific regulatory responsibilities are handled by five centers: the Center for Biologics Evaluation and Research, the Center for Devices and Radiological Health, the Center for Drug Evaluation and Research, the Center for Food Safety and Applied Nutrition, and the Center for Veterinary Medicine. A sixth center, the National Center for Toxicological Research, conducts scientific research and provides expert technical advice and training that inform FDA's science-based regulatory decisions.

The House and Senate Appropriations subcommittees on agriculture have jurisdiction over FDA's appropriations. FDA's budget consists of two types of funds: public funds appropriated by Congress (called budget authority or direct appropriations) and private (i.e., industry) funds (called user fees)

FDA-RELATED ISSUES

FDA-related issues of interest to Congress generally rest on the central question of how best to give people access to useful products while protecting them from unsafe ones. Creating too many regulatory requirements raises costs and prevents products from reaching consumers. Creating too few places consumers at risk [1].

The 110th Congress placed a new focus on FDA's regulatory responsibilities, passing the most comprehensive FDA reform legislation in almost a decade: the Food and Drug Administration Amendments Act of 2007 (FDAAA; PL 110-85) [2]. FDAAA reauthorized four expiring programs and expanded the agency's authority to regulate the safety of prescription drugs and biologics, medical devices, and foods. In the wake of that legislation, issues remain both in areas that FDAAA did not comprehensively address and in areas raised by its implementation. The following is an introduction to the types of issues that Congress now faces with respect to FDA. For further assistance with any FDA-related issue, see Table 3 (at the end of the report) for a list of CRS experts.

Budget. The primary budget-related question faced by Congress is how to fund the agency sufficiently for it to carry out its responsibilities, while also funding competing national needs, and ensuring that the agency operates cost-effectively [3].

Table 3. CRS Experts

Area	Analyst(s) and Phone Number(s)
FDA Team Leader	Erin D. Williams (7-4897)
Foods	Donna V. Porter (7-7032), Geoffrey S. Becker (7-7287)
Human Drugs	Susan Thaul (7-0562)
Biologics	Judith A. Johnson (7-7077)
Animal Drugs and Feeds	Sarah A. Lister (7-7320)
Devices and Radiological Health	Erin D. Williams (7-4897)
Blood and Plasma Products	C. Stephen Redhead (7-2261)
Human Cellular and Tissue Products	Bernice Reyes-Akinbileje (7-2260), Erin D. Williams (7-4897)
Legal Issues	Vanessa K. Burrows (7-0831)

Some secondary budget-related questions center on user fees.4 They ask to what extent FDA should be funded by money from the industries it regulates, and for which activities such funds should be collected and used (e.g., premarket review, inspection and enforcement).

Premarket Approval. Before FDA will permit drugs, devices, and biological products to be marketed in the United States, the agency requires evidence that they are safe and effective. (Only limited types of food ingredients require premarket approval.) Premarket approval processes vary by product type [5]. Most processes rely on evidence from clinical trials. The topic of clinical trials raises questions of when it is appropriate to test new products on people, particularly on children, and in what circumstances it is appropriate to publicize the trials and their results [6].

The approval process for new products can take time. While this may be of little consequence for people with manageable conditions, special issues arise for people with life-threatening diseases or conditions for which there is no current treatment. As a result, some interest has been focused on mechanisms for giving people access to unapproved medications, and for speeding FDA's approval process [7].

Products on the Market. FDA is responsible for ensuring the safety of products it regulates — including foods — once they are on the market. It accomplishes this goal through product tracking, inspection, and enforcement. Some attention has been focused on the fact that the agency has different enforcement authorities for product types. For example, FDA has mandatory recall authority for medical devices and infant formula, but not for other foods or for prescription drugs [8]. Questions have also arisen regarding whether marketing with FDA approval should preempt certain tort claims [9].

FDA's role dovetails with product safety issues that cut across numerous agencies, creating the need for interagency coordination [10]. For products such as tobacco and genetic tests, the current patchwork of regulation — or lack thereof — has led to calls for comprehensive FDA oversight [11]. In areas of shared responsibility, such as product importation and advertising, FDA's role, and its ability or willingness to use agency resources to fulfil its responsibilities, has caused concern [12].

Food Safety. As noted above, there is no premarket approval for foods or most food ingredients. FDA's statutory authority and historical approach are reactive, focused on foods or ingredients that are found to be unsafe [13]. Many policy makers seek a more preventive approach and debate how to craft such a system. Proposals include having FDA inspect processes instead of products, set performance measures, or increase industry's burden to assure safety. A successful approach may take into account the variety of foods FDA regulates, a growing stream of imported foods, limited global food tracking systems, and the agency's finite resources.

Advisory Committees. In its vetting of the numerous products it regulates, FDA relies on non-binding input from groups of outside experts known as advisory committees. Because the experts in specialized fields may often be those with a financial stake in the resulting products, questions have emerged about managing conflicts of interest in the advisory committees [14].

Products and Technologies. Questions have been raised about FDA's ability to keep up with the increasing sophistication of some types of products it regulates, such as genetic tests, follow-on (generic) biologics, and cell- and tissue-based products [15]. A similar concern has been raised about its ability to assess health threats that may arise from combined exposures to multiple types of FDA-regulated products, and other exposures [16]. Others have focused on politically sensitive products, such as the contraceptive "Plan B" [17]. There are also questions about the adequacy of FDA's assessment of the safety of products produced using emerging technologies, such as biotechnology [18]. All of the above questions are intensified for combination products — those composed of two or more regulated components (e.g., a drug/device, or a biologic/device) — whose regulation requires coordination across FDA centers.

REFERENCES

[1]   See CRS Report RL33802, *Pharmaceutical Costs: A Comparison of Department of Veterans Affairs (VA), Medicaid, and Medicare Policies,* by Gretchen A. Jacobson, Sidath Viranga Panangala, and Jean Hearne, and "Drugs, Biologics, and Medical Devices," CRS CLI, at [http://apps.crs.gov/cli/cli.aspx?PRDS_CLI_ITEM_ID=2678&from=3&fromId= 13].

[2]   See CRS Report RL34465, *FDA Amendments Act of 2007 (P.L. 110-85),* by Erin D. Williams and Susan Thaul, and CRS Report RS22779, *Food Safety: Provisions in the Food and Drug Administration Amendments Act of 2007,* by Donna V. Porter.

[3]   See CRS Report RL34334, *The Food and Drug Administration: Budget and Statutory History, FY1980-FY2007,* by Judith A. Johnson, Donna V. Porter, Susan Thaul, and Erin D. Williams, and CRS Report RL34638, The FDA FY2009 Budget, by Judith A. Johnson, Sarah A. Lister, Donna V. Porter, Pamela W. Smith, Susan Thaul, and Erin D. Williams.

[4]   See CRS Report RL33914, *The Prescription Drug User Fee Act (PDUFA): History, Reauthorization in 2007, and Effect on FDA,* by Susan Thaul (hereinafter RL33914); CRS Report RL34571, *Medical Device User Fees and User Fee Acts,* by Erin D. Williams; and CRS Report RL34459, Animal Drug User Fee Programs, by Sarah A. Lister (hereinafter RL34459).

[5]   See RL33914; RL34459; and CRS Report RL32826, *The Medical Device Approval Process and Related Legislative Issues,* by Erin D. Williams (hereinafter RL32826).

[6]   See CRS Report RL32909, *Federal Protection for Human Research Subjects: An Analysis of the Common Rule and Its Interactions with FDA Regulations and the HIPAA Privacy Rule,* by Erin D. Williams; CRS Report RL33986, *FDA's Authority to Ensure That Drugs Prescribed to Children Are Safe and Effective,* by Susan Thaul; and CRS Report RL32832, *Clinical Trials Reporting and Publication,* by Erin D. Williams.

[7]   See CRS Report RS228 14, *FDA Fast Track and Priority Review Programs,* by Susan Thaul.

[8]   See CRS Report RL34167, *The FDA's Authority to Recall Products,* by Vanessa K. Burrows.

[9]   See Riegel v. Medtronic, Inc. (552 U.S. __ (2008); No. 06-179 (U.S. February 20, 2008)).

[10] See "Product Safety Authorities and Remedies," CRS CLI, at [http://apps.crs.gov/cli/   cli.aspx?PRDS_CLI_ITEM_ID=3   1 17&from=3&fromId= 13].

[11] See CRS Report RL326 19, *FDA Regulation of Tobacco Products: A Historical, Policy, and Legal Analysis,* by C. Stephen Redhead and Vanessa K. Burrows; CRS Report RL33719, *Tobacco: Selected Legal Issues,* by Vanessa K. Burrows; CRS Report RS22944, *Federal Trade Commission Guidance Regarding Tar and Nicotine Yields in Cigarettes,* by Vanessa K. Burrows; and CRS Report RL33832, *Genetic Testing: Scientific Background for Policymakers,* by Amanda K. Sarata (hereinafter RL33832).

[12] See CRS Report RL32191, *Prescription Drug Importation and Internet Sales: A Legal Overview,* by Vanessa K. Burrows; CRS Report RS2 1711, *Legal Issues Related to Prescription Drug Sales on the Internet, by Vanessa K. Burrows;* and RL32826.

[13] See CRS Report RS22600, *The Federal Food Safety System: A Primer,* by Geoffrey S. Becker and Donna V. Porter, and "Food Safety and Nutrition," CRS CLI, at [http://apps.crs.gov/cli/ level_2.aspx?PRDS_CLI_ITEM_ID= 13].

[14] See CRS Report RS22691, FDA Advisory Committee Conflict of Interest, by Erin D. Williams.

[15] See RL33832; CRS Report RL34045, *FDA Regulation of Follow-On Biologics,* by Judith A. Johnson; CRS Report RL33901, *Follow-On Biologics: Intellectual Property and Innovation Issues,* by Wendy H. Schacht and John R. Thomas; CRS Report RL34614, *Nanotechnology and Environmental, Health, and Safety: Issues for Consideration,* by John F. Sargent; CRS Report RL34332, *Engineered Nanoscale Materials and Derivative Products: Regulatory Challenges,* by Linda-Jo Schierow; CRS Report RL3 3540, *Stem Cell Research: Federal Research Funding and Oversight,* by Judith A. Johnson and Erin D. Williams; and CRS Report RL3 3554, *Stem Cell Research: Ethical Issues,* by Erin D. Williams and Judith A. Johnson.

[16] See CRS Report RL34572, *Phthalates in Plastics and Possible Human Health Effects,* by Linda-Jo Schierow and Margaret Mikyung Lee, and CRS

Report RS22869, *Bisphenol A (BPA) in Plastics and Possible Human Health Effects,* by Linda-Jo Schierow and Sarah A. Lister.

[17] See CRS Report RL33728, *Emergency Contraception: Plan B*, by Judith A. Johnson and Vanessa K. Burrows.

[18] CRS Report RL3 3334, B*iotechnology in Animal Agriculture: Status and Current Issues*, by Geoffrey S. Becker and Tadlock Cowan.

INDEX

A

academic, 49
access, 11, 54, 56, 85, 87, 95, 97
accountability, 5
accuracy, 4, 8, 18, 19, 23, 33, 48, 53, 60, 61
administration, 50, 62
administrative, 6, 40
Administrative Procedure Act, 89
adults, ix, 2, 84
adverse event, 15
advertising, 15, 71, 92, 98
advisory committees, 98
agricultural, 21, 28, 31
agriculture, 95
aid, 82, 84
allergens, 13, 25, 31, 33, 34, 35
alternatives, 73
American Cancer Society, 61
American Heart Association, 43, 47, 61
amino, 88
amino acid, 88
amino acids, 88
appendix, 39, 50, 58, 74
appropriations, 95
Appropriations Committee, 39
assessment, 6, 36, 38, 86, 98
auditing, 7, 62
Australia, 21, 28, 32
authority, ix, 6, 10, 38, 39, 40, 41, 50, 53, 55, 84, 85, 87, 93, 95, 96, 97, 98

availability, 72

B

benchmarks, 43
benefits, 40, 44, 50, 83, 85
binding, 98
biotechnology, 98
bioterrorism, 37
Bioterrorism Act of 2002, 39, 41
Bisphenol A (BPA), 101
bleaching, 52
blood, 14, 51, 92
Brazil, 21, 32
Bureau of Alcohol, Tobacco, Firearms and Explosives, 92

C

calorie, 51
Canada, 11, 13, 21, 28, 31, 32, 43, 44, 46, 48, 61
capacity, 4
Capacity, 86
carbohydrates, 43, 47
catfish, 31
cell, 98
certification, 41, 47
childhood, ix, 2
children, 47, 97
Chile, 21, 32

China, 21, 28, 32
cholesterol, 43, 51
chronic disease, 3
chronic diseases, 3
clinical trial, 97
clinical trials, 97
Co, 34
codes, 35
coding, 35, 57
collaboration, 12, 54
Columbia, 73
commerce, 15, 26, 27, 41
Committee on Appropriations, 1, 2, 86
communication, 5, 57, 72
compliance, 4, 5, 11, 14, 16, 18, 21, 23, 29,
    31, 33, 34, 54, 56, 82
components, 92, 99
confusion, 11, 54
Congress, iv, x, 6, 12, 13, 35, 41, 42, 53, 55,
    57, 70, 71, 92, 95, 96
Connecticut, 61
consent, 27, 87
constraints, 22, 52
consulting, 11, 44, 47
consumers, ix, 3, 4, 6, 10, 12, 13, 26, 34, 37,
    41, 42, 43, 44, 45, 47, 48, 49, 50, 51, 54,
    55, 57, 59, 82, 84, 85, 95
consumption, 48, 50, 85
contracts, 4, 64
corn, 52
cosmetics, 4, 92
cost-effective, 96
costs, 37, 39, 95
country of origin, 21, 32
Court of Appeals, 71
courts, 27
CRS, x, 91, 92, 96, 99, 100, 101
customers, 40

decision making, 33
decisions, 9, 12, 34, 47, 52, 56, 57, 83, 84, 95
defense, 40, 57, 82
definition, 6, 51, 59
demand, 36
density, 44, 50
Department of Agriculture, 2, 3, 60, 93
Department of Health and Human Services, x,
    2, 3, 91
detention, 28, 39, 41, 84, 87
diabetes, ix, 2
diet, 3, 43, 50
dietary, 3, 6, 13, 23, 25, 26, 27, 59, 70, 71, 72,
    87, 88
dietary supplement labeling, 70
diets, 14
disability, 3
diseases, 97
distribution, 4, 58
District of Columbia, 71, 73
District of Columbia Circuit, 71
draft, 11, 33, 35, 42, 50, 55, 57
Drug Enforcement Administration, 92
drugs, x, 22, 27, 91, 92, 93, 96, 97
drying, 52
duplication, 35

E

eating, 43
Education, 2, 70, 86, 94
egg, 93
employees, 37
encouragement, 51
Environmental Protection Agency, 93
EPA, 88, 92, 93
equity, 6, 40
erosion, 5
Europe, 42, 43
European Commission, 11, 44, 47, 61
European Union, 44, 47
exercise, 15, 72, 73
expenditures, 5
expert, iv, 95
expertise, 41, 44, 49

D

data collection, 12, 56, 84
database, 9, 16, 23, 24, 25, 26, 34, 35, 57, 60,
    61
death, 3, 34, 41

exposure, 55

F

failure, 28
fat, 3, 13, 15, 19, 30, 46, 47, 50, 51
fats, 46
fatty acids, 43
FDA, vii, ix, x, 1, 2, 3, 4, 5, 6, 7, 8, 9, 10, 11,
   12, 13, 14, 15, 16, 17, 18, 19, 20, 21, 22,
   23, 24, 25, 26, 27, 29, 31, 32, 33, 34, 35,
   36, 37, 38, 39, 40, 41, 42, 43, 44, 48, 49,
   50, 51, 52, 53, 54, 55, 56, 57, 59, 60, 61,
   62, 63, 64, 66, 67, 68, 69, 70, 71, 72, 73,
   82, 83, 84, 85, 86, 87, 88, 89, 91, 92, 93,
   94, 95, 96, 97, 98, 99, 100
FDA approval, 97
February, 23, 26, 27, 100
federal government, 85
Federal Register, 70
Federal Trade Commission (FTC), 2, 7, 61,
   92, 100
fee, ix, 39
fees, 6, 10, 39, 53, 55, 70, 83, 87, 95, 97
fiber, 13, 46
finance, 37, 38
firms, ix, x, 4, 7, 8, 10, 16, 18, 22, 34, 37, 39,
   40, 41, 52, 59, 62, 63, 64
First Amendment, 71, 72, 84
fish, 28, 31
focus group, 51
focus groups, 51
food, ix, 3, 4, 5, 6, 7, 8, 9, 10, 11, 12, 13, 14,
   15, 16, 18, 19, 21, 22, 23, 25, 26, 27, 28,
   29, 30, 31, 32, 33, 34, 35, 36, 37, 38, 39,
   40, 41, 42, 43, 44, 46, 47, 49, 50, 51, 52,
   53, 54, 55, 56, 57, 59, 60, 61, 62, 63, 70,
   71, 72, 82, 83, 84, 85, 86, 87, 88, 93, 97, 98
Food and Drug Administration (FDA), vii, ix,
   x, 1, 2, 3, 58, 59, 74, 91, 94, 95, 99
food industry, 16, 40, 46
food products, 8, 15, 18, 19, 33, 49
food programs, 10
food safety, ix, 4, 5, 9, 11, 36, 37, 40, 55, 56,
   57, 82, 93

foreign firms, 8, 40, 62
fraud, 71
Freedom of Information Act, 23
fructose, 52
fruit juice, 30
fruits, 3, 86
FTC, 2, 15
funding, 7, 9, 12, 37, 60, 83, 96
funds, 95, 97

G

General Mills, 50
ginseng, 25
goals, 38, 55, 71
government, 5, 7, 10, 43, 49, 62, 71, 85, 89
Government Accountability Office, vii, 1
grading, 41
grain, 48, 50
grains, 3, 48, 50
group work, 48
groups, 3, 4, 7, 11, 43, 52, 61, 98
growth, 8, 48
GSA, 69
guidance, 3, 4, 5, 7, 8, 50, 60, 72, 74, 89
guidelines, 3

H

handling, 4, 15
harm, 34
health, ix, 3, 6, 7, 10, 11, 14, 22, 23, 25, 31,
   34, 41, 42, 43, 44, 46, 47, 48, 49, 51, 54,
   55, 56, 59, 61, 62, 70, 71, 72, 73, 82, 83,
   85, 87, 89, 98
Health and Human Services (HHS), x, 2, 3,
   58, 70, 86, 91
health problems, ix
healthfulness, 85
hearing, 11, 48
heart, 3, 46, 47, 51
Heart, 43, 46, 47, 61
heart disease, 3, 51
HHS, x, 2, 3, 39, 44, 55, 81, 82, 84, 86, 91, 92

high blood pressure, 14
high risk, 34, 83
HIPAA, 99
Hong Kong, 21, 32
House, 1, 2, 46, 95
human, x, 91, 92, 94

I

id, 38, 70
identification, 55
identity, 25, 30
illegal drug use, 92
imitation, 25
implementation, 12, 55, 70, 74, 96
imported article, 84
importer, 5, 27
imports, 7, 19, 21, 27, 28, 31, 32, 36, 37, 41,
    59
incentive, 40
incidence, 2
India, 33
Indonesia, 21, 31
industry, 3, 4, 6, 7, 10, 16, 40, 46, 49, 54, 62,
    82, 95
infants, 88
inflation, 37
information systems, 33
information technology, 5, 36, 83
infrastructure, 5
injunction, 5, 27, 87
injuries, 41
injury, iv, 15
Innovation, 100
inspection, 4, 10, 15, 16, 18, 26, 37, 40, 41,
    82, 94, 97
Inspection, 2, 7, 60, 93
inspections, x, 4, 8, 10, 11, 16, 18, 23, 27, 40,
    53, 56, 60, 64, 83
inspectors, ix, 39, 40, 53, 55
instruments, 62
insurance, 93
Internet, 100
interstate, 27, 41
interstate commerce, 27, 41

interviews, 7
investigative, 12, 56, 84
investment, 35, 83, 84
iron, 22
Italy, 21, 31

J

January, 5, 7, 9, 33, 62, 71, 85
jobs, 12, 56, 84
jurisdiction, 8, 15, 17, 41, 95
justification, 87

L

labeling, ix, 3, 4, 6, 7, 8, 9, 10, 11, 12, 13, 15,
    16, 18, 19, 22, 23, 24, 26, 27, 28, 29, 30,
    31, 32, 33, 34, 35, 36, 37, 38, 39, 41, 42,
    43, 44, 46, 47, 49, 50, 51, 52, 53, 54, 55,
    56, 57, 59, 60, 61, 70, 71, 72, 82, 83, 86,
    87, 88
language, 42, 73, 85, 86
law, 19, 53, 62, 73, 93
laws, ix, 11, 82, 93
lawsuits, 71
LDL, 51
legislation, 47, 71, 95
legislative, 39
life-threatening, 13, 97
likelihood, 6, 53
limitations, 33, 57, 61
lipoprotein, 51
livestock, 41
location, 25, 30
long-term, 73

M

Macau, 21, 32
magnetic, iv
management, 5, 54, 56, 84, 88
manufacturer, 25, 27, 30
manufacturing, 18, 40
market, 48, 97

marketing, 97
meals, 3
measures, 98
meat, 41, 52, 93
Medicaid, 93, 99
medical products, 10
Medicare, 93, 99
medications, 97
memorandum of understanding, 15
Mexico, 21, 28, 31
milligrams, 14
minerals, 19, 44
misleading, ix, x, 3, 4, 6, 8, 10, 11, 13, 15, 16,
    24, 30, 39, 42, 47, 49, 50, 52, 54, 55, 59,
    60, 61, 71, 74, 83, 84, 85
missions, 36
money, 97
mushrooms, 27

N

national, 40, 47, 96
National Highway Traffic Safety
    Administration, 41
natural, 51
Netherlands, 44, 45, 46, 61
New York, iii, v, 61
Nicotine, 100
NLEA, 2, 70, 71, 73
non-binding, 98
nutrient, 8, 13, 14, 15, 21, 25, 31, 44, 48, 49,
    59, 60, 70, 89
nutrients, 3, 8, 13, 14, 15, 19, 21, 43, 48, 50,
    51, 86
nutrition, 3, 7, 11, 13, 16, 18, 19, 25, 28, 30,
    42, 43, 44, 47, 48, 50, 51, 54, 55, 57, 62,
    85, 88
Nutrition Labeling and Education Act, 2, 70
nuts, 13, 35

O

obesity, ix, 2, 82

Offices of Congressional Relations and Public
    Affairs, 58
oil, 26
oils, 52
Omega-3, 88
online, 24, 60
organization, 49
organizations, 6, 10, 40, 42, 43, 44, 46, 47, 49,
    59
oversight, ix, 4, 5, 7, 10, 12, 16, 23, 33, 36,
    39, 52, 59, 60, 82, 83, 98
overweight, ix, 2

P

peanuts, 13
perceptions, 10, 39
performance, 7, 62, 98
periodic, 55, 57
permit, 52, 71, 97
pesticides, 93
pharmaceuticals, 62
PL, 95
planning, 37
policy makers, 3, 98
poultry, 41, 52, 93
power, 92
prejudice, 72
prescription drug, 92, 96, 97
prescription drugs, 96, 97
preservative, 30
preservatives, 25, 34
pressure, 14
preventive, 98
preventive approach, 98
priorities, 6, 9, 11, 22, 33, 52, 54, 56, 59, 82,
    83
private, 95
probability, 34
program, 3, 33, 34, 35, 36, 40, 41, 53, 69
proliferation, 48
promote, 3, 47
property, iv
protocol, 87

public, 2, 4, 5, 9, 11, 12, 16, 23, 34, 36, 38, 39, 40, 41, 43, 48, 50, 53, 54, 55, 56, 57, 61, 71, 72, 82, 83, 84, 85, 87, 95
public funds, 95
public health, 2, 4, 11, 23, 38, 39, 41, 43, 56, 71, 72, 82, 83
Public Health Service, 93
Puerto Rico, 86

Q

qualifications, 12
quality assurance, 35

R

Radiation, 93, 94
random, 18, 19
range, 10, 21, 92
recall, 4, 16, 35, 41, 60, 97
red light, 46
regulation, 11, 55, 62, 70, 71, 72, 73, 89, 98, 99
regulations, ix, 4, 5, 6, 11, 13, 14, 15, 18, 23, 27, 49, 54, 56, 60, 62, 70, 71, 73, 74
regulatory requirements, 95
relationship, 14, 43, 70, 73, 89
relationships, 14
reliability, 7, 23, 35, 36, 61
rent, 69
research, 10, 11, 12, 39, 43, 44, 47, 48, 51, 57, 62, 83, 85, 89, 95
resolution, 34
resource allocation, 12
resources, ix, 5, 6, 9, 10, 11, 12, 33, 35, 36, 38, 39, 40, 41, 42, 49, 52, 53, 54, 55, 56, 57, 59, 83, 84, 98
responsibilities, ix, 9, 11, 33, 36, 37, 38, 52, 53, 55, 56, 82, 83, 93, 95, 96, 98
revenue, 6, 40, 48
risk, 3, 12, 14, 34, 51, 56, 83, 95

S

safety, 4, 5, 11, 22, 36, 38, 42, 53, 56, 72, 82, 92, 96, 97, 98
sales, 46, 48
salt, 3, 46, 47
sample, 21
sampling, 8, 18, 19, 62
saturated fat, 46, 47, 50
school, 3
scientists, 11, 44
seafood, 23, 28, 31
searches, 62
security, 37
seizure, 5
seizures, 7, 9, 22, 26, 59, 60
selecting, 35
Senate, 86, 94, 95
September 11, 37
services, iv
skills, 37
sodium, 13, 14, 46
soil, 15
specificity, 37
staffing, 7, 9, 37, 39, 59, 60, 83
stakeholder, 7
stakeholders, 6, 10, 12, 42, 44, 47, 48, 49, 50, 51, 54, 55, 57, 59, 82, 85
standards, 7, 46, 62, 70, 71, 72
Standards, 45, 52
stars, 48
statistics, 12, 55
statutes, 4, 5, 6, 54, 56, 60
statutory, 10, 23, 42, 55, 56, 70, 98
statutory provisions, 23
strategies, 6, 43, 53, 62
strength, 73
stroke, 3
sugar, 3, 15, 19, 43
sugars, 46, 47
sulfites, 13, 31
supervision, 88
supplements, 6, 23, 27, 59, 71, 72, 86, 87
supply, 5, 37, 42, 53
sustainability, 5

Sweden, 11, 44, 45, 46, 61
symbols, 10, 12, 42, 43, 44, 47, 48, 54, 57, 62
symptoms, 55
synthesis, 43, 87
systems, 11, 33, 35, 43, 44, 47, 49, 56, 84, 98

T

Tea, 88
technical assistance, 42
Texas, 61
Thailand, 21, 31
threat, 41
threatened, 72
threats, 6, 37, 98
time, 2, 9, 12, 16, 26, 35, 37, 43, 48, 54, 55,
    56, 57, 58, 61, 84, 97
time frame, 54, 55, 57
tissue, 98
tobacco, 69, 97
tort, 97
total costs, 37
total product, 29
toys, 92
tracking, 12, 34, 54, 56, 83, 97, 98
trading, 42
trading partners, 42
traffic, 45
training, 70, 84, 95
trans, 30, 50
transformation, 5
transparent, 73
transplantation, 93

Treasury, 92
Treasury Department, 92

U

U.S. Department of Agriculture(USDA), 2, 3,
    60, 93
uniform, 10, 42, 43
United Kingdom, 11, 32, 44, 45, 48, 61
United States, 3, 4, 5, 8, 10, 17, 18, 27, 28, 42,
    43, 47, 49, 88, 97
updating, 22, 72
USDA, 2, 3, 5, 41, 44, 52, 86, 93

V

validity, 35, 36
values, 15, 43, 51
variables, 15
vegetables, 3, 86
vitamin A, 21
vitamin C, 22
vitamins, 13, 19, 22, 43, 44

W

warning letters, x, 5, 7, 8, 9, 12, 16, 22, 23,
    24, 25, 26, 34, 52, 54, 57, 59, 60
water, 92
whole grain, 3, 48, 50
Wisconsin, 61